Patterns and Portraits:
Women in the History
of the
Reformed Church in America

edited by
Renée House
John Coakley

The Historical Series of the Reformed Church in America

No. 31

Patterns and Portraits:
Women in the History
of the
Reformed Church in America

edited by
Renée House
John Coakley

Wm. B. Eerdmans Publishing Co.
Grand Rapids, Michigan

Dedicated to
Carol W. Hageman
whose years of faithful servant leadership
in the church and
at New Brunswick Theological Seminary
have produced fabulous fruits
and opened the way of ministry
for women and men,
clergy and lay persons alike.

Body text set in Adobe New Caledonia.
Chapter titles set in in Adobe Garamond.

Contents

Acknowledgments

We gladly express our thanks to several people whose help has been invaluable: to John W. Beardslee III and Mary Kansfield, who, as members of the committee on the Standing Seminar in RCA History at New Brunswick Theological Seminary, did much to develop the 1994-95 lecture series in which the first versions of most of the essays were presented publicly; to Beverly Sullivant, who prepared the initial typescript; to Joyce Goodfriend, who advised us wisely at a very difficult juncture in the project and generously worked on our behalf; to Norman Kansfield, who has given his unqualified support at every turn; and especially to Russell Gasero, who has cheerfully aided the project in innumerable ways, not least by his skillful work in readying the volume for press, on behalf of the Historical Commission. Finally, we gratefully acknowledge a substantial financial contribution from New Brunswick Theological Seminary — drawn in part from the Archibald Laidlie Fund — to help underwrite the costs of publication.

R.S.H.
J.W.C.

Preface

This book has had a long, slow, complicated, and apparently inevitable birth. Most of the essays included here were first conceived and delivered as lectures or talks in the Standing Seminar in Reformed Church History at New Brunswick Theological Seminary from 1994-1995. The original decision to focus the seminar on the history of women in the RCA was motivated by a desire to bring to light the hidden stories of the church's women, to recognize the depth and breadth of their contributions, and to acknowledge the denomination's continuing struggle to understand fully and embrace women's gifts for the church and its members.

But the goal of the seminar was not simply to tell the untold stories of women or to give voice to their concerns in the church. Rather, the goal was, through the exploration of women's history and experience in the RCA, to begin more fully to tell the whole story of this North American denomination. By recounting the history of women in the RCA, we do more than tell the other half of the story—at least potentially, we begin to rewrite the entire story as it has been told to date. By adding the history of women, we will slowly shift perspective on the whole history of the RCA, and, we might even say, on the history of the Protestant church in America. Writing "women's history" is akin to adding one color of paint to another—in the end, one creates an entirely different color.

This book is but a small contribution to the larger enterprise of writing the church's history. Even as we celebrate the contents of this volume, we are mindful of what is not included here, of all that must still be investigated and brought into print. As part of the seminar, Dr. Sara Smith, an African-American lay woman, reminisced about more than twenty years as an active member of the church. Dr. Smith's firsthand account of the formation of the denomination's Black Caucus and her reflections on the experience of African-Americans in a predominantly white denomination highlighted the need for further inquiry into these aspects of women's experience in the RCA. We had hoped to include Dr. Smith's presentation among these essays, but it was her desire to augment her reflections with further historical research before bringing them to print. We can look forward to the fruits of her labors.

We had also hoped this collection would include works focused on the history and experience of Pacific-Asian, Native American, and Latina women in the RCA. The church's racial/ethnic councils worked diligently to support this effort, beginning with the planning of the standing seminar six years ago. Unfortunately, constructing the hidden history of women in these traditionally underrepresented groups takes an enormous amount of time and energy—more than any single person was able to devote in the face of lecture and publishing deadlines. However, in the process of seeking to include these voices, we have uncovered enough interest to cause us to envision a companion volume to this one in which the stories of all the church's women can be more fully recounted.

This volume appears at a time when the RCA is mandating that students preparing for ministry be helped to understand the important contributions women have made throughout the church's history, and the particular role they have played in the history of the RCA. We trust that these essays, in their great variety, will open doors to a largely unknown and unexplored past, and that they will spark further inquiry into the history of Christian women.

Another significant initiative accompanies the publication of these essays—that is, the reorganization of women's ministries within the RCA. These changes are prompted by many factors, two of which stand out. The first is that the needs, expectations, and patterns of participation of lay women in the denomination have changed dramatically, while the organization intended to serve them has changed relatively little. As a result, only 14 percent of the church's women participate in the organization intended to serve and empower them.

The second factor is that the ordination of women to all church offices that began more than twenty-five years ago shifted church structures relating to women. In 1973, the Rev. Joyce Stedge was the first woman ordained to the ministry of Word and sacrament in the RCA. She graciously offered her reflections on these painful, pioneering times as part of the Standing Seminar Series on the History of Women in the RCA. Ms. Stedge's ordination was challenged by some in the church, and triggered a series of events that forced the denomination finally to reach a settlement on the question of women's ordination to all offices (see further John Coakley's "Introduction"). In time, the Commission on Women was created to serve the needs and track the presence of women in ordained offices, and to raise consciousness throughout the RCA concerning the ordination of women. The existence of two organizations for women in the church—one focused on lay, the other on ordained women—has resulted in a sometimes unhelpful separation of women's ministries in the denomination.

Diana Paulsen, executive director of Reformed Church Women from 1986 to 1994, acknowledged this reality when she spoke in the seminar five years ago. In that presentation, she courageously told the truth of women in the RCA as she experienced it through her work with women throughout the church. Ms. Paulsen's presentation was not primarily historical, so is not included here, but by speaking out, she provided a powerful of reminder of two things: how much work must still be done toward the full inclusion of women in the church's ministries, and how faithfully women have and continue to serve the church, despite many, many obstacles.

Recognizing this reality, we rejoice in the birth of this book which demonstrates historically the breadth and depth of women's participation in the work of the church, from the spiritual and religious formation of children to the ministries of preaching, teaching, and evangelism. By faithfully fulfilling the roles assigned them by church and society, and by resisting these roles to enter new ones, women have unalterably shaped the reality of the church. In the pages that follow, we offer a glimpse into this truth and dare to hope that such seeing will make a difference for the RCA, and for the greater church as well.

I
Women in the History of the Reformed Church in America

John W. Coakley

This volume of essays presents a variety of explorations into the history of women in the Reformed Church in America (RCA).[1] The present essay, by way of introduction, attempts an overview of the subject, with reference to the other essays in the volume and to some other scholarship as well. The overview has two parts, for I want to suggest that the history of women within the denomination be approached through two different (though not completely mutually exclusive) lines of investigation. One of these inquires

---

1. As a study of the history of women in an American denomination, this volume joins a shelf already occupied by several useful books, including: Hilah F. Thomas and Rosemary Skinner Keller, eds., *Women in New Worlds* (Nashville: Abingdon, 1981) [on Methodist women]; Catherine M. Prelinger, ed., *Episcopal Women: Gender, Spirituality, and Commitment in an American Mainline Denomination*, (New York: Oxford University Press, 1992); Evelyn Brooks Higgenbotham, *Righteous Discontent: The Women's Movement in the Black Baptist Church, 1880-1920* (Cambridge: Harvard University Press, 1994); and Lois A. Boyd and R. Douglas Brackenridge, *Presbyterian Women in America: Two Centuries of a Quest for Status*, 2nd ed. (Westport, Connecticut: Greenwood Press, 1996).

into women's place in the church's *organizational* life; the other inquires into their place in its *extraorganizational* life.

Those terms first require explanation. By "organizational life" I mean all the worship, mission, and education, and the articulation of belief, that are accomplished through its institutions and officers. By "extraorganizational" life, I mean the whole life experience of persons—individuals, families, and groups—insofar as that experience affects or is affected by their shared faith, beliefs, concerns, and values as members of the church.

It is not unusual to focus upon the organizational life of the church (in the sense of the definition above) when one writes church history. That is probably what the reader expects. In the case of women, although there is much to be said about their organizational contributions that has not been said before, saying it does not require a basic change in the *way* we approach the church's history. But in order to bring women's full contributions potentially into view, it is necessary to venture into the church's extra–organizational life (in the sense of my definition) as an aspect of its history too. Such a venture, by contrast to the "organizational" approach, may rightly strike the reader as unusual. It is, moreover, a venture that challenges us to broaden our usual way of thinking about the history of the RCA more generally, and perhaps also our way of thinking about the denomination as it exists today.

Women and the Organization

To begin with women's part in the "organizational" life of the RCA: their emergence as officials and otherwise as leaders with responsibility for its institutions, is something that has come about slowly, and not particularly smoothly, over a long period time.

Here a word is in order about the general shape of the written history of the RCA. The denomination has taken a particular pride in its history—which is usually traced to the arrival of the first Dutch Reformed minister in New Netherland (Jonas Michaelius) in 1628, and, beyond that, to the Dutch Reformation—and has fostered a distinguished body of historical literature. The monuments of that literature include several one-volume histories, E.T. Corwin's *Digest of Synodical Legislation* (1906), the same author's massive *Manual of the Reformed Church in America* (five editions between 1859 and 1922), and the volumes of the Historical Series of the RCA, which was begun in 1968 under the auspices of the denomination's

Historical Commission and now comprises a substantial collection of monographs, source collections, reference works, and anthologies of essays, including the present volume.[2] Much of this literature, like the historical literature of most other denominations, takes as its subject what I am calling the "organizational" sphere of the church's life. The great events of this literature are the establishment of Dutch congregations in the colonial period, the long and initially divisive eighteenth-century struggle to attain independence from the Classis of Amsterdam and yet maintain the Dutch Reformed structures and confessions, the establishment of theological seminaries and colleges, the mid-nineteenth-century union of many of the then-new midwestern Dutch Reformed immigrants with the old eastern churches of colonial descent, the subsequent secession of some of these new members, the establishment and support of foreign missions, the deeds of missionaries, the processes of Americanization of language and custom, the proposals for merger with other bodies, the perennial reorganization of bureaucracies, the debates and pronouncements of the General Synod.

With a few exceptions, that traditional historiography has had very little to say about women. The reason is, in a certain sense anyway, clear enough: that it was only very recently (through a set of events to which I shall return) that women have become eligible to hold the constitutional offices of the church, namely the offices of minister of the Word (or as we now say, of Word and sacrament), elder, deacon, and professor. For most of the denomination's history women were excluded from those offices, and consequently in all that time the debates and actions of the official bodies

2. The one-volume histories include: David Demarest, *History and Characteristics of the Reformed Protestant Dutch Church* (New York, 1856); Edward T. Corwin, et al., *A History of the Reformed Church, Dutch, the Reformed Church, German, and the Moravian Church in the United States* (New York: Christian Literature Company, 1895); Willard Dayton Brown, *A History of the Reformed Church in America* (New York: Board of Publication and Bible School Work, 1928); *Tercentenary Studies of the Reformed Church in America* (New York: Reformed Church in America, 1928); Howard G. Hageman, *Lily Among the Thorns* (n.p.: Reformed Church Press, 1953); Arie Brouwer, *Reformed Church Roots* (n.p.: Reformed Church Press, 1978). Corwin's *Digest*, as well as his *Manual* in its five editions (1859, 1869, 1879, 1902, 1922) and one supplement (1933) was published by the denomination's Board of Publication in New York, and the Historical Series of the Reformed Church in America has been published from the outset by W. B. Eerdmans in Grand Rapids. A helpful review of RCA historiography is: Lynn Japinga, "The Glue That Holds Us Together: History, Identity, and the Reformed Church in America," *Reformed Review* 45 (1992):181-201.

of the church, from the General Synod to the local consistories—and therefore the events that have constituted the church's story as we are accustomed to tell it—have been the province of men. And for this reason, although of course none of our historians in past generations sat down to write with the conscious thought, "I am only going to speak about *men* here," in effect that is what the great majority of them have done.

In fact, however, women do have a place in the "organizational" history of the RCA. This is true not only in the sense that in the mid- to late-twentieth-century women have gained authorization to hold constitutional offices, but also in the sense that, once we have those gains in mind, we see that the groundwork was laid for them by some developments that stretch back into the nineteenth century. The events by which these changes came about constitute an episode that can be comfortably added to the familiar list of the church's other formative episodes—an important chapter in the denomination's history that in itself requires no major reconceptualizing of that history.

We can distinguish three parts to the story of women's emergence in the "official" arena of the church—parts that overlap somewhat chronologically, but when presented in sequence give evidence of a continuous, if not smooth, process: first, the rise and partial demise of official organizations that were supervised by women specifically for "women's work," over the period from the mid-nineteenth century to the present; second, the emergence and firm establishment of women in the official role of missionary, over roughly the same period of time; and third, the twentieth-century struggle, eventually successful, for the authorization of women's ordination.

"Women's Work" and the "Parallel Church"

During the course of the nineteenth century in the RCA, as in other denominations, there developed what the historian Joan Gundersen has called the "parallel church."[3] This was the constellation of women's organizations, mostly focused on mission, that came to exist within a given

3. Joan R. Gundersen, "Women and the Parallel Church: A View from Congregations," in *Episcopal Women*, ed. Catherine M. Prelinger, pp. 111-132, insightfully traces the emergence of a women's "separate sphere" in the Episcopal Church in the nineteenth century, and the demise of that separate sphere in the early twentieth. See also Mary Sudman Donovan, "Beyond the Parallel Church: Strategies of Separatism and Integration in the Governing Councils of the Episcopal Church," ibid., pp. 133-163.

denomination at every level from the local to the national. These were organizations that ostensibly existed to support the mission work of the denomination, and in no way challenged its male leadership, but on the other hand they also provided a space in which women could exercise their own leadership.[4]

In the RCA, at the national level, the "parallel church" first emerged in the formation of the Woman's Board of Foreign Missions (WBFM) and the Women's Executive Committee of the Board of Domestic Missions (WEC) in 1875 and 1882 respectively, which were staffed by women. But its grassroots origins may be found somewhat earlier, on the local and classical level, where women had already been organizing to support missions for several decades, as Russell Gasero says in his essay in this volume. Once organized, the national organizations capitalized on such women's energies by raising money through auxiliary societies in local churches, specifically for mission work among women and children. They also encouraged women to take on new leadership roles, as Renee House shows in her analysis of the journal, the *Mission Gleaner*, which the WBFM published from 1883 to 1917. House finds the *Gleaner*'s writers using stories of biblical women to call attention to the importance of women's contributions and making use of the venerable "cultural assumption" that women's area of influence was the home to motivate their readers to support women's missionary work that was clearly outside the home, such as the Ferris Academy for girls in Japan. These national women's mission agencies were expressing and stimulating, as Gasero says, a "slow understanding that women have a job to do, gifts to share, and a call to answer" beyond their traditional domestic sphere.

In the twentieth century, the "parallel church" has been widely challenged in American denominations, and the RCA has been no exception. By the mid-twentieth century, and in some denominations even by the end of the nineteenth, the existence of separate women's missions organizations was being called into question, and most denominations moved to disband

4. For a detailed account of the emergence of such female leadership among the Presbyterians, see Page Putnam Miller, *A Claim to New Roles* (Metuchen: Scarecrow Press, 1985). See also Boyd and Brackenridge, *Presbyterian Women*, 3-49. For the Methodists (among whom such women's organizations emerged, but who constitute a special case, as having also fostered female preaching), see Jean Miller Schmidt, "Denominational History When Gender Is the Focus: Women in American Methodism," in *Reimagining Denominationalism: Interpretive Essays*, ed. Robert Bruce Mullin and Russell E. Richey (New York: Oxford University Press, 1994), pp. 203-221.

separate women's mission boards at the national level. The ostensible reason has been their gender-divisiveness; thus in the 1920s the Presbyterian mission executive Robert Speer asked,

> If we have in our churches women's organizations, what have we got? Haven't we got two churches? We have one church made up of men and women, with a social program, an educational program, and a religious program. Then we have a separation of women, with identical programs, except worship. We do not want to divide what is spoken of as "the church" and "the women." The great danger is that the women will think that their society is the only thing they have to work over.[5]

The sincerity of such concern is not necessarily to be doubted, and Speer himself consistently advocated the ordination of women among the Presbyterians long before it was officially authorized. But historians have also suggested that male leaders' discomfort with the real power that the women's groups were exercising by virtue of the large amounts of money they were raising contributed to the demise of women's boards of missions; and although upon the demise of those boards women typically received seats on the central denominational boards to which they had formerly been auxiliary, they nonetheless constituted minorities on those central boards. Thus, though mission governance became truly gender inclusive, paradoxically women also lost opportunities for leadership.[6] The RCA seems to have been typical in this regard, as Carol W. Hageman's essay in this volume shows. The WBFM and the WEC survived the Second World War but then were merged into the denomination's other mission agencies shortly afterward, ostensibly for considerations of finance and efficiency but with the effect, as Hageman argues, of a subtle but real disempowerment of women—a disempowerment only partially offset, she thinks, by the denomination's later approval of women's ordination.

A Woman as Missionary

If the mission-oriented "parallel church" has provided nineteenth- and twentieth-century women one set of opportunities to acquire roles of

5. Quoted in Boyd and Breckenridge, *Presbyterian Women*, p. 31.
6. See for instance Boyd and Breckenridge, *Presbyterian Women*, pp. 24-37; Gundersen, "Women and the Parallel Church," pp. 122-124.

Christian leadership within the institutional cadres of the church, the mission fields themselves have provided them another. Already in 1836 among the missionaries sent to Borneo, women figured in the first foreign mission established under the direct auspices of the RCA—and not only the spouses of the male missionaries, but also a single woman, Azubah Condict[7]; and a steady stream of women followed into foreign mission in subsequent years. The much-revered position of missionary may be seen as something approaching, in practice if not in legal fact, an *office* in the church; and thus missionary women became, in a certain sense, the church's first female office-holders, long before women were eligible to serve as ministers, elders, deacons, or professors.

It is in perhaps because of this effectively official status of missionaries, and a certain authority that arises from it, that among all the existing studies of the denomination's history, it is in the history of mission that women have been most conspicuous. For instance in the recent comprehensive histories of the RCA missions to Arabia and China by Lewis Scudder and Gerald De Jong, respectively, the contributions of women, even though not signaled as a subject in their own right, often appear as a matter of course.[8] It is also the case that, aside from the recent rich collection of short biographies of women by Una Ratmeyer, the most extensive biographical literature about RCA women to date has been a quartet of memoirs by female missionaries—Dorothy Van Ess, Jeanette Boersma, Cornelia Dalenberg, and Mary Bruins Allison, all of the Arabian mission.[9] In the present volume, Jennifer Reece explores the nature of a female missionary's authority in her essay on the remarkable Sara Couch, who served in Japan from 1892 to 1946. She shows that Couch, though hardly someone of overbearing personality, did much

---

7. Eugene Heideman, *A People in Mission: The Surprising Harvest* (n.p.: Reformed Church Press, 1984), p. 6.
8. Gerald F. De Jong, *The Reformed Church in China 1842-1951*, HSRCA no. 22 (Grand Rapids: Eerdmans, 1992); Lewis R. Scudder, *The Arabian Mission's Story: in Search of Abraham's Other Son*, HSRCA no. 30 (Grand Rapids: Eerdmans, 1998).
9. Una H. Ratmeyer, *Hands, Hearts and Voices: Women Who Followed God's Call* (New York: Reformed Church Press, 1995); Dorothy F. Van Ess, *Pioneers in the Arab World*, HSRCA no. 3 (Grand Rapids: Eerdmans, 1974); Cornelia Dalenberg, *Sharifa*, HSRCA no. 11 (Grand Rapids: Eerdmans, 1983); Jeanette Boersma, *Grace in the Gulf*, HSRCA no. 20 (Grand Rapids: Eerdmans, 1991); Mary Bruins Allison, *Doctor Mary in Arabia: Memoirs by Mary Bruins Allison, M.D.* (Austin: University of Texas Press, 1994).

to shape her own ministry, in no small part because of her "professional training" and the "intellectual achievement" that her missionary appointment both presupposed and built upon.

Women in Office

Although RCA women were therefore already assuming public leadership roles in the so-called parallel church and in the mission fields even in the nineteenth century, not until the twentieth century was there any concerted effort to open to women the constitutional offices of the church.

Once mounted, the effort took many years. On the question of women's eligibility to become elders and deacons, it was in 1918 that the General Synod first received an overture to change the *Book of Church Order* to allow women to be elected to those offices. The synod rejected the overture, and subsequent synods rejected similar overtures in 1921, 1932, 1936, 1945 and 1951. Finally the synod of 1952 voted for the change, but the action did not receive the necessary subsequent approval of two-thirds of the classes, and similar synod actions in 1958, 1965 and 1967 met the same response. Two-thirds approval finally came after the 1971 synod, and so it was in the following year, 1972—fifty-four years after the first overture—that the synod declared women eligible for the offices of elder and deacon.[10]

As for the discussion of women's eligibility for the office of minister of the Word, it did not last quite as long as the discussion about elders and deacons; the General Synod began addressing the question of women's ordination as ministers in 1955, and the conclusion was reached in 1979. Yet even so the debate about this issue could hardly be called brief, and it was surely more intense and heated. The tangle of events surrounding it was particularly complex; a detailed account is beyond the scope of this introduction, and at any rate can be found elsewhere.[11] Suffice it to say here that the issue was finally resolved as a "judicial" rather than a "constitutional" matter. For although the ministry had always been assumed to be a male preserve, the *Book of Church Order* in fact defined ministers in an implicitly gender-inclusive way as "those persons who have been inducted into that office by

10. Edwin G. Mulder, "Full Participation—a Long Time in Coming!," *Reformed Review* 42 (1989):227-31.
11. Mulder, "Full Participation," pp. 231-37; Allan J. Janssen, *Gathered at Albany*, HSRCA no. 25 (Grand Rapids: Eerdmans, 1995), pp. 136-46; Daniel J. Meeter, *Meeting Each Other*, HSRCA no. 24 (Grand Rapids: Eerdmans, 1993), pp. 13-17.

ordination…"; and when a series of synod actions in the 1970s to make that inclusiveness explicit by changing the word "persons" to the words "men and women" failed to win approval of two-thirds of the classes, several Eastern classes proceeded to act on the assumption that "persons" indeed meant both women and men. Thus between the synod of 1978 and that of 1979, four women were actually ordained by their classes. A fifth—Joyce Borgman de Velder, whose essay in this volume covers these events from an autobiographical perspective—received classis approval, but her actual ordination was still pending at the time the 1979 synod met. Complaints against these classes' actions were made to the synod of 1979, which then proceeded to consider the matter as judicial business—that is, as a matter of interpreting rather than changing the *Book of Church Order*. This meant that it was no longer necessary to secure agreement from two-thirds of all classes; now all that was needed was a majority vote of the synod to deny the complaints and thereby sanction the ordination of women. That majority was readily obtained.[12]

In spite of the decision of the General Synod of 1979, however, the movement to open the constitutional offices of the church to women has been in several ways inconclusive. As Joyce de Velder remarks in her recollection of the events of 1979, even amidst her "relief and gratitude" at the decision of the synod, she was painfully aware that many persons remained opposed. The following year the General Synod, in response to widespread complaint about the action of 1979, approved and sent to classes two "conscience clauses" to be added to the *Book of Church Order* stipulating that classis members could not be required to participate in "the licensure, ordination or installation of women…contrary to their consciences," and exempting ministers from being "pressured" to "offend against…conscience," and all church members from being penalized for "conscientious objection" on this issue. After approval by two-thirds of the classes, these clauses became part of the *Book of Church Order* in 1981.[13] Thus it remained, and remains, permissible to oppose the ordination of women. Women are indeed preparing for ministry in the RCA in significant numbers, as illustrated by Mary Kansfield's essay here describing the

12. Mulder, "Full Participation," pp. 231-37.
13. *Minutes of the General Synod*, 1980, p. 275; Renee House, "Matters of Conscience, Compromise or Coercion: Thoughts on the 'Conscience Clause,'" paper presented to the Standing Seminar in RCA History at New Brunswick Seminary, 1993.

experiences of the female candidates for the Master of Divinity at New Brunswick Seminary, where in 1994 they accounted for 42 percent of RCA students. But employment rates for women in local parish ministry appear to be still low; and the acceptance of women as elders and deacons is still not universal.[14]

Women and the Whole Christian Life

I have so far presented a brief sketch of the important and complex story of the emergence of women within the "organizational" life of the RCA. It is a story that merits much more research at every point, and one that needs to be added to—or rather, woven into—our established narrative of the organizational life of the RCA, so that women lose their invisibility there. It is also, however, a story that belongs naturally within the familiar organizational mode of denominational history yet in fact; and as signaled at the outset of this essay, I want to suggest that it is as much—or really, more— in the *extra*organizational sphere that we discover the real historical importance of women in the church's history. And so I turn to that extra-organizational sphere.

Here a comment is first in order about what it is we mean when we speak of a "denomination." Recent scholarship that has documented the changing face of denominationalism in America, such as the work of Wade Roof, William McKinney, and Robert Wuthnow, has made clear that the average American's sense of identity with a given denomination is far weaker now than it was fifty years ago.[15] The differences in denominations' confessions and institutions—the distinctives, that is, of what I am calling broadly their "organizational" life—have drastically decreased in their importance as

14. The "Directory of Ordained Women in the Reformed Church in America" as updated August, 1997, lists 136 ordained women, of whom 72 were serving in parish ministry (either as pastors, co-pastors, associate pastors, or ministers under contract). On the service of women as elders and deacons, the report of the Commission on Women to the 1998 General Synod shows the denominational average percentage of women on consistories to be 26.5, with significant regional variation: consistories in the West and Canada follow the denominational average, while those in the East are higher and those in the Midwest lower. *Minutes of the General Synod*, 1998, p. 353. Mulder, "Full Participation," pp. 238-44, gives an earlier (1989) statistical appraisal.

15. Wade Clark Roof and William McKinney, *Amerian Mainline Religion* (New Brunswick: Rutgers University Press, 1987); Robert Wuthnow, *The Restructuring of American Religion* (Princeton: Princeton University Press, 1988).

factors motivating and defining people's religious commitments. And yet denominations evidently persist, with apparently increasing self-awareness and concentration on planning for their own futures, often in ways that do not conspicuously display their own distinctiveness from other denominations so much as they attempt to appeal to perceived needs and dispositions of potential members. In such a situation, as Nancy Ammerman has pointed out, we realize that the very meaning of "denomination" is elusive and complex.[16] How is one to say what gives a denomination its particular identity? If the answer cannot be found so clearly in the apparent distinctiveness of its beliefs and institutions as was once the case, we must look more broadly to the whole lives of its members, to see the ways in which the denomination touches them and is touched by them. Inevitably, we will bring the same sensibility to the denomination's past.

Such considerations by themselves indicate the importance of going beyond the organizational sphere when we think about a denomination. The need to make women visible is surely another reason for doing so; for although, as we have seen, women's struggle for a place in the official institutions of the church has been slow and relatively recent, there is no question that women have always held membership in the church in great numbers. It is true that in the extraorganizational sphere the differences between one denomination and another may be not be clear at all, as is suggested by John Beardslee, who argues in his essay in this volume that the place of women in Dutch-American communities has not differed greatly from their place in other American communities. It is also true that methodological problems arise when we try to find out about the lives of these women; the sources that inform us of the domestic life are rather different from those that inform us of the public life of church officials, and often more difficult to evaluate.[17] And sometimes, as in the case of Christina Van Raalte presented by Karsten Rumohr-Voskuil and Elton Bruins in their

16. Nancy Ammerman, "Denominations: Who and What are We Studying?," *Reimagining Denominationalism,* pp. 111-133.
17. It may be that a certain conservatism allied to the concern to preserve ethnic tradition or identity has contributed to the denomination's slowness in recognizing the ordination of women. For a parallel case of a mid-twentieth-century struggle for women's ordination, in this case among Lutherans of Scandinavian and German background, see L. DeAne Lagerquist, *From Our Mothers' Arms: A History of Women in the American Lutheran Church* (Minneapolis: Augsburg Press, 1987), esp. chapter 5.

essay, the very obscurity of domestic life may prevent us from knowing much of what we want to know about a given woman. Yet, as several of the essays here will suggest, the problems are often not insurmountable, and many sources as yet untapped have much to tell us. At any rate, once we do shift our focus from the organizational to the extraorganizational sphere, women suddenly become very visible indeed.

The essays in this volume that focus on the extraorganizational life of the church demonstrate women's historic visibility particularly in two roles: first, the role of guardian and transmitter of the faith within the family, and second, the role of exemplar of piety.

As for the first of these roles—the role of domestic transmitter of the faith—it may not surprise the reader to be told that women have had such an influence, since women still in late twentieth-century America widely fill that role, This is a phenomenon with deep roots in Christian history, and perhaps in human society itself. As the 19th-century French historian Michelet wrote, "Every woman is a school, and it is from her that the generations truly acquire their belief. Long before the father gives any thought to an education, the mother has conveyed her own, and it will not wear off."[18] The very fact that we assume that women will fill some such role is part of the reason that we do not think to notice it. On the other hand, the very rootedness of the phenomenon in our culture gives evidence of its importance. The essays here give evidence both of its important influence and of its potential to change over time—change that reveals much about the experience of the people of the church. Joyce Goodfriend's discussion of Dutch women in the colonial period presents various evidence of women's religious influence in the family and household, such as the telling notations in men's wills of contributions to church on wife's behalf and the striking seventeenth-century correspondence between Jeremias van Rensselaer and his mother Anna, in which we see the mother "urging him to live up to religious precepts" and the son responding by, among other things, choosing a wife in his mother's pious mold. Later, by the mid-nineteenth century, the RCA, like the dominant evangelical culture of which it was a part, had developed a full-fledged ideology of Christian motherhood whereby, as Firth Haring Fabend's essay here shows, a woman

18. Quoted by Jean Delumeau, "Préface," in *La religion de ma mère: Les femmes et la transmission de la foi*, ed. Jean Delumeau (Paris: Cerf, 1992), p. 11.

had the responsibility of "anguishing over her children's spiritual welfare," and more specifically the job of seeing to it that her children were "saved"; ministers, moreover, typically recollected their own mothers' influence with great emotion, and mothers were widely exhorted to make their sons into ministers. It would seem to be no exaggeration to say that within the home, everyone (men and women alike) assumed that women were the real evangelists, in a more clearly defined sense than anything Goodfriend's colonial sources reveal.

The degree to which that ideal of evangelical motherhood has survived into the late twentieth century in the RCA, and the ways in which it may have evolved, are subjects that would repay further study. The emphasis that Mary Kansfield's essay places on the personal sacrifices that female students make to attend New Brunswick Seminary puts one in mind of the self-sacrificial mode of the ideal as described by Fabend and raises the question to what extent ordained women carry—or are expected to carry—with them into the realm of their ecclesiastical office the ancient domestic female roles that used to be explicitly nonofficial.

The second role I wish to call attention to—the role of women as exemplars of piety, figures in whom the belief of the church became distinctively concretized—is not unrelated to the first. For, as some of the evidence of Fabend and Goodfriend would suggest, the importance women were assumed to have as Christian educators in the home in former centuries was not simply a function of their greater proximity to children (although that was certainly part of it) but also a function of the high degree of piety that they were also assumed to have, implicitly often greater than that of the men of the family. The figure of Dina van den Bergh, the eighteenth-century woman whom Johan Van de Bank discusses in his essay here, offers a striking example of such piety. Van den Bergh was born in the Netherlands in 1725, came to New Jersey in 1750 and was the wife, successively, of two prominent Reformed church pastors. In the letters and diary fragments that survive from her, we see a woman of strong personality and profound piety, with a sophisticated personalized understanding of the teachings that she received from certain identifiable pietistic ministers. She also possessed an extremely acute—to a modern reader, often exhausting—spiritual self-consciousness. And although we would need much more comparative evidence to be able to discern in what sense, if any, such self-consciousness was distinctively female at the time, still it is evident from the sources that Dina, to whom ministers came for advice, was a formidable and widely revered figure.

It must be admitted that the various pieces of evidence our essays give about the piety of women in the history of the Reformed Church in America are not adequate to establish patterns in that piety, or demonstrate how it may have varied according to time and circumstance. But the evidence is extensive enough to make clear that women served as influential figures of piety long before they acquired any offices or organizational positions in the church; and when we have a fuller picture of the history of piety in this denomination, we can expect that women will have a large place there.

The very idea of investigating the extraorganizational history of the denomination requires us, at any rate, to explore some unfamiliar territory, and in the process to employ questions and sources rather different from those of the more familiar "organizational" mode of denominational history. This is particularly evident in the essay of Goodfriend, who, finding the classic sources such as sermons and synodical documents generally useless for answering her questions about women in the colonial Dutch churches, demonstrates the usefulness of a fascinating array of other sources instead, including paintings, wills, and church subscription lists. In a similar way, Fabend and House make productive use of highly conventional Sunday school publications that would be of no value at all as sources for a narrative of events. For to understand the extraorganizational life of the church the crucial thing is not so much to ask about events, or turning points, or even about the great issues of the day, but about how the witness of the church— and specifically of this denomination—shapes the whole lives of its members, and how, conversely, those whole lives might shape the denomination.

Women's History and Denominational History

The essays that follow, taken together, illustrate in detail the breadth of the history of women in the Reformed Church in America as I have tried to sketch it here, embracing both the organizational and the extraorganizational spheres of the life of the church. These essays limit themselves to the subject of women. But by way of conclusion I suggest that by its very breadth this project of a history of women in the Reformed Church in America also poses a challenge for our conception of the denomination's whole past, and indeed of its present. Without for a moment losing sight of the schisms and mergers, the initiatives of leaders and groups, the establishment of institutions, the great debates of synods, and so on, the study of women's history teaches us that the question, "What are the great events in this denomination's history and why have they come about?" must never stand alone. If that is the only question we ask, we take too restricted a view of that mysterious living entity, a denomination. We leave too many people out. Instead, another question must always complement it, namely the question, "What has it *meant* to be part of this denomination?"—a question that requires us to seek access to the very souls of those who belong or have belonged to it, whether they were obscure or prominent, lay or clerical, articulate or silent, female or male.

II
Incorporating Women Into the History of the Colonial Dutch Reformed Church: Problems and Proposals

Joyce D. Goodfriend

In November 1749, a botanist from Sweden named Peter Kalm attended morning and afternoon worship in New York City's Dutch Reformed church. A meticulous observer, he recorded every detail of the services in his journal and gave descriptions of the city's Dutch church buildings as well. At three points in his journal entry, he made mention of women. In the Old Dutch Church, which he attended in the afternoon, he noted, "There were large balconies, and it was the custom here that the men sat there while the women occupied the ground floor, except the pews against the walls which were reserved for the men." Women also played a part in the service that afternoon. "As soon as the sermon was finished and the minister had read a few prayers, a woman carrying a child on her arm came forward to the pulpit. Then the minister began to read from there all the prayers [for the occasion] contained in the Dutch prayer book, and when he had finished she took the child to the rector, who sat in his pew, and let him christen it." In the morning, at the New Dutch Church, the attire of female churchgoers had caught Kalm's eye. "The women as a rule had black velvet caps which

16

they could fasten on by tying at the ears. Others wore the ordinary English gowns and short coats of broadcloth, of various colors. Nearly everyone had her little container, with the glowing coals...under her skirt in order to keep warm."[1]

The women of New York City's Dutch Reformed church were visible to Peter Kalm in the mid-eighteenth century. The location of their seats in the church edifice, their appearance, and their role in the sacrament of baptism all elicited comment from him. But female churchgoers have been all but invisible to denominational historians, whose gaze has been more on the pulpit than the pews. Wedded to a conception of history that places the beliefs and actions of leaders at its center, historians of the colonial Dutch Reformed church have trained their sights on the men who formulated church policy—ministers and members of the consistory.[2] Women, rendered incapable of filling leadership roles in church life by their presumed intellectual inferiority and their expected subordination to their husbands and fathers, are absent from these accounts.[3]

From the perspective of the 1990s, this appears to be a narrow and limiting vision of church history, one that is increasingly untenable in light of the social and cultural changes of the last thirty years as well as the ongoing reconceptualization of colonial religious history. American women's quest for fuller and more equal participation in American society in the past few decades has resulted in some remarkable alterations in social arrangements and attitudes. Religious institutions have not been immune from the pressures for change, and while their responses have varied, each has sought to meet the challenges posed by the contemporary social upheaval. In the

1. Adolph B. Benson, ed., *The America of 1750: Peter Kalm's Travels in North America. The English Version of 1770.* 2 vols. (New York, 1966; originally published 1937). II, p. 624.
2. Though there are entries for Blacks and Indians, there is no entry for women in the index of Gerald F. De Jong, *The Dutch Reformed Church in the American Colonies* (Grand Rapids, Mich., 1978).
3 For an initial effort to rectify this imbalance, see Joyce D. Goodfriend, "Recovering the Religious History of Dutch Reformed Women in Colonial New York," *de Halve Maen*, lxiv (Winter 1991), pp. 53-59. Historians of the Reformed church in the seventeenth-century Netherlands also confront the problem of incorporating women into the church's history. See Mirjam De Baar, "'Let Your Women Keep Silence in the Churches'. How Women in the Dutch Reformed Church Evaded Paul's Admonition, 1650-1700," in W. J. Sheils and Diana Wood, eds., *Women in the Church. Papers Read at the 1989 Summer Meeting and the 1990 Winter Meeting of the Ecclesiastical History Society* (Oxford, 1990), pp. 389-401.

process of rethinking current practices, they have been impelled to reflect on the record of the past. As they do this, denominational historians can draw lessons from historians of American religion who are working toward a more encompassing model of church history.

Casting the history of the colonial Dutch Reformed church in a more inclusive mold requires moving beyond a clergy-centered view of the church. Analyses of sermons must be coupled with attempts to discern how auditors understood these sermons. Disputes between ministers and their congregations must be examined from the point of view of churchgoers as well as the minister. Incorporating the laity into church history involves recognizing that congregants were not an undifferentiated group. Attention must be paid to the rank and file of churchgoers as well as to those of high social status, to females as well as to males, and to people of all ethnic backgrounds.[4] One cannot hope to recapture the individuality of more than a few members of the colonial Dutch Reformed church, but it is possible to obtain a clear picture of the various types of congregants.

According the laity a more prominent place in denominational history entails modifying the traditional institutional view of church history. Ordinary men and women had full lives and as a rule spent only the Sabbath at church. But this did not mean that the Reformed faith was peripheral to their lives. What is needed, then, is a community-based history of the Reformed Dutch in colonial America that looks not only at the church, but at husbands and wives, parents and children, and slave masters and slaves. In this newly wrought denominational history, women will emerge from culturally constructed oblivion to parts of great significance, if not to leading roles.

The study of women in colonial American religion has been a vital field of inquiry in recent years. When one surveys this expanding literature, one is struck by the proliferation of studies of Puritan and Quaker women.[5] These

---

4. For recent and more inclusive approaches to the historical study of American congregations, see the essays in James P. Wind and James W. Lewis, eds., *American Congregations,* 2 vols. (Chicago and London, 1994). Also relevant in this connection are Jon Butler's comments on the "astonishing vacuum in our knowledge of lay religious behavior" in early America. Jon Butler, "The Future of American Religious History: Prospectus, Agenda, Transatlantic Problematique," *William and Mary Quarterly,* 3rd Series, 42 (1985), pp. 167-183. (Quote on 170.)
5. For useful guides to this literature, see Gerald F. Moran, "'The Hidden Ones': Women and Religion in Puritan New England" in Richard L. Greaves, ed., *Triumph Over Silence: Women in Protestant History* (Westport, Conn., 1985), pp. 125-149; and Mary Maples Dunn, "Latest Light on Women of Light" in Elisabeth Potts Brown and Susan Mosher Stuard, eds., *Witnesses For Change: Quaker Women over Three Centuries* (New Brunswick, N.J., 1989), pp. 71-85.

studies rest, in part, on social analysis, but their true underpinning is the rich repository of personal documents left by the female members of these churches. The well known propensity of Puritans and Quakers, male and female, to chart their spiritual lives has proved a bonanza to historians seeking to introduce gender as a category of analysis into studies of early American religion. Scholars of Puritan and Quaker women, working with journals and conversion narratives, have significantly advanced our understanding of the stages of spiritual growth their subjects went through and, in the process, explored the ramifications of gender in early American religious history.

But Dutch Reformed women in the middle colonies of New York and New Jersey do not seem to have had a rationale for chronicling their religious experiences and thus have left us hardly any written records of their inner life. This does not mean that their spiritual journeys were any less complex than their counterparts in New England and Pennsylvania or that they did not undergo inner turmoil as they sought to affirm their faith.

To gain a sense of what is missing in our documentation of the lives of colonial Dutch Reformed women, one can turn to the religious biographies of Reformed women that appear in the journal of Jasper Danckaerts, a Labadist missionary who toured New York in the late seventeenth century. Despite Danckaerts's sectarian slant, these profiles hold special interest because they are highly particularized. One records the experiences of a French woman, Marie Renard Cresson, who was a member of the Dutch Reformed church at Harlem in upper Manhattan. According to Danckaerts, who met her in 1680, she "had undergone, several years ago, some remarkable experiences; of a light shining upon her while she was reading in the New Testament about the sufferings of the Lord Jesus, which frightened her very much. It did not continue long but soon passed off; yet it left, nevertheless, such a joy and testimony in her heart as she could not describe. She kept it to herself, without making it known to any one except one woman. Some years afterward, while lying abed in the morning, she heard a voice which said to her she must make this glory known, which she did do to Dominie Nieuwenhuise [the minister of New York City's Dutch Reformed Church], who told her he did not know what to say." Then, a man whom Danckaerts called "a false teacher" attempted to dissuade her from going to church and participating in communion. "This has...sorely disturbed this poor woman...for not to go to church, and to leave the Lord's Supper, she could

not in her heart consent."6 Danckaerts and his missionary colleague went on
to give spiritual counsel to Marie Cresson.

If historians of the Dutch Reformed church had more such biographical
sketches, or better still, if they had firsthand accounts by Reformed women
of their interior life, then the task of weaving the female perspective on
church life into the denominational record would be far simpler. But we are
faced with a paucity of documents pertaining to the spirituality of colonial
Dutch Reformed women. Our challenge is to delineate the contours of
Dutch Reformed women's religious life without recourse to personal
writings resembling those of Puritan and Quaker women. In practical terms,
this entails adopting a combination of tactics—extracting meaning from
every shred of available literary evidence, making creative use of behavioral
evidence, supplementing information on colonial Dutch women with material
drawn from the history of Reformed women in the Netherlands, and, when
necessary, clarifying the experiences of Dutch Reformed women by referring
to those of women in other colonial denominations. This rather eclectic
strategy must serve in lieu of more conventional methods, given the dearth
of personal documents produced by Dutch colonial women. I will give an
idea of what can be learned from this approach and, in so doing, suggest
some avenues for future research.

I would like to start with a visual image drawn from seventeenth-century
Dutch art—a woman holding or next to a Bible.7 This convention was
carried over from the Netherlands to the Dutch settlements in America,
where artists depicted women with the Bible as well.8 These portraits
obviously suggest that spiritual concerns were of major importance to
Dutch women. On a more mundane level, the image of a woman holding the
Scriptures also suggests that Dutch women possessed Bibles and were in the
habit of Bible reading. An examination of colonial wills and inventories of
estates, as well as surviving artifacts, makes clear that Dutch women had

6. Bartlett Burleigh James and J. Franklin Jameson, eds., *Journal of Jasper
    Danckaerts, 1679-1680* (New York, 1913), pp. 231-232. See also Danckaerts's
    account of Elizabeth van Rodenburgh's spiritual quest. Ibid., pp. 145-146; 170.
7. For examples, see Wayne E. Franits, *Paragons of Virtue: Women and Domesticity
    in Seventeenth-Century Dutch Art* (Cambridge, 1993), pp. 163, 164.
8. For examples, see Roderic H. Blackburn and Ruth Piwonka, *Remembrance of
    Patria: Dutch Arts and Culture in Colonial America 1609-1776* (Albany, 1988),
    pp. 60, 61, 217.

their own Bibles, distinct from the large family Bibles owned by most colonial Dutch Reformed families.[9] Psalters containing the New Testament and the psalms were carried to church by Dutch Reformed women.[10] It was exceptional for a woman to inherit the family Bible—this occurred only when there were no male heirs—but occasionally women recorded family events in the great Bible.

That the contents of the Bible were well known to Reformed women in the colonies is suggested by the effortlessness with which scriptural passages were cited by Maria van Cortlandt van Rensselaer, the widow of Jeremias van Rensselaer, in her correspondence with family members.[11] In perusing these seventeenth-century letters, one gets the impression of a common religious vocabulary shared by Maria and her correspondents on both sides of the Atlantic. No doubt many other Dutch colonial women could also cite scriptural passages with ease. But any attempt to generalize about how widespread knowledge of the Bible was among colonial Dutch Reformed women must ultimately confront the issue of literacy. Scholars now know that far more colonial women could read than write, so that the existence of a substantial segment of the female Dutch colonial population which could not write—these women signed legal documents with a mark—does not necessarily prove that many women were unable to read.[12] Though our evidence is fragmentary, it seems likely that colonial Dutch women of even modest social standing were capable of reading the Bible.[13] The frequency with which Bibles are noted in the wills and inventories of ordinary people

9. Joyce D. Goodfriend, "Probate Records as a Source for Early American Religious History: The Case of Colonial New York City, 1664-1730," Paper delivered at the Dublin Seminar for New England Folklife, 1987.
10. Alice P. Kenney, "Neglected Heritage: Hudson River Valley Dutch Material Culture," *Winterthur Portfolio*, 20 (Spring 1985): 67. See also Alice P. Kenney, "Hudson Valley Psalmody," *The Hymn*, 25 (1974): 15-26.
11. A.J.F. van Laer, transl. and ed., *Correspondence of Maria van Rensselaer 1669-1689* (Albany, 1935). For commentary, see Goodfriend, "Recovering the Religious History of Dutch Reformed Women," pp. 55-56.
12. E. Jennifer Monaghan, "Literacy Instruction and Gender in Colonial New England," *American Quarterly*, 40 (1988): 18-41. The standard, but now outdated, treatment of literacy in early New York is William Heard Kilpatrick, *The Dutch Schools in New Netherland and Colonial New York* (Washington, D.C., 1912).
13. According to Anne Grant, girls in early eighteenth-century Albany "were taught...to read in Dutch, the bible and a few Calvinist tracts of the devotional kind...few were taught to write." [Anne Grant], *Memoirs of an American Lady: With sketches of Manners and Scenery in America, as They Existed Previous to the Revolution*. 2 vols. (New York, 1970; originally published 1808) vol. 1, p. 33.

points to this conclusion. So does an incident that occurred in New Amsterdam in 1655. A young girl was captured by Indians, who gave her two inexpensive Bibles which they had taken from a home in New Amsterdam. When the girl was returned to the settlement, she wished to keep the Bibles, which had provided her with spiritual comfort during her ordeal. However, the housewife whose property they were sued for their return and won her case.[14] A legal battle between female adversaries over two small Bibles: what better evidence can be adduced to demonstrate that women had the ability to read the Scriptures?

Along with reading the Bible and perhaps some devotional works, Dutch Reformed women undoubtedly included prayer in their daily routine. Praying by individuals in Dutch Reformed households was too ordinary to provoke comment, but a chance reference by Maria van Cortlandt van Rensselaer to the fact that her father died while in his prayers is a rare illustration of this habit.[15] Prayer also had an important place at family meals. The midday meal was represented in the art of the Netherlands as a religious occasion. The theme of the family saying grace was familiar in Dutch paintings, where families were shown as praying before they commenced eating.[16] In 1744, Dr. Alexander Hamilton, a Scottish physician from Maryland who was touring the northern colonies, described, in a rather condescending fashion, the mealtime behavior of some Dutch women on Staten Island.

"As I sat down to dinner I observed a manner of saying grace quite new to me. My landlady and her daughters put on solemn, devout faces, hanging down their heads and holding up their hands for half a minute. I…sat staring at them with my mouth choak full, but after this short meditation was over, we began to lay about us and stuff down the fryed clams with rye-bread and butter."[17] Though Hamilton downplays the sanctity of the moment, one must not overlook the significance of this injection of the sacred into the daily routine.

14. Ellis Lawrence Raesly, *Portrait of New Netherland* (New York, 1945), pp. 257-258.
15. "Maria van Rensselaer to Richard van Rensselaer, November 12, 1684," *Correspondence* of Maria van Rensselaer, p. 173.
16. Franits, *Paragons of Virtue*, pp. 143-154. See also Wayne Franits, "The Family at Grace: A Theme in Dutch Art of the Seventeenth Century," *Simiolus*, 16 (1986): pp. 36-49.
17 Carl Bridenbaugh, ed., *Gentleman's Progress: The Itinerarium of Dr. Alexander Hamilton, 1744* (Chapel Hill, 1948), pp. 39-40.

Saying grace at mealtimes was undoubtedly a commonplace occurrence among colonial Dutch Reformed families as was the practice of fathers reading the Bible to the assembled household and possibly the singing of the beloved psalms. That these Dutch Reformed traditions escaped mention merely indicates how deeply embedded they were in family routines.

Dutch Reformed women contributed to the spiritual life of the household in numerous ways, but it was in the roles of wife and mother that they played their most critical part in sustaining their family's religious identity. Through example, a pious wife could set standards of behavior for her spouse that might eventually lead to his confessing his faith and becoming a church member. One measure of wives' influence over their husbands might be to take a sample of female church members and compare the dates of their admission to the church with those of their husbands. Ascertaining the proportion of husbands who joined after their wives gives an indication of the influence exerted by women on their mates.

Well aware of their husbands' control over family economic resources, wives may have found it necessary to cajole their husbands to set aside money for the Dutch Reformed church. Reserving small sums for the weekly collection may not have been a problem, but to persuade their husbands to contribute to the building fund may have required considerable skill on the part of wives, especially when husbands were not church members. An examination of the list of contributors to the 1688 fund for building a Dutch Reformed church in New York City reveals several instances in which a man's contribution, whether in money or in kind, was explicitly noted as being for his wife.[18] That husbands felt obliged to carry out their wives' wishes when it came to charity for the church is perhaps best illustrated by the donation in 1656 of twenty-five florins to the deacons of the Beverwijck Dutch Reformed Church "from Goosen Gerritsen, being money which his wife has promised to the poor on her death bed."[19]

18. Kenneth Scott, "Contributors to Building of a New Dutch Church in New York City, 1688," *National Genealogical Society Quarterly*, 49 (1961), pp. 131-136. See also Randall H. Balmer, *A Perfect Babel of Confusion: Dutch Religion and English Culture in the Middle Colonies* (New York, 1989), pp. 100-101.
19. A.J.F. van Laer, "Deacon's Account Book, 1652-1664," The Dutch Settlers Society of Albany *Yearbook*, 7 (1931-1932): 7. For an overview of charitable giving in the Dutch Reformed church in Beverwijck and Albany, see Janny Venema, "'For the Benefit of the Poor': Poor Relief in Albany/Beverwijck, 1652-1700," M.A. Thesis, State University of New York at Albany, 1990.

If a wife could convince her husband to part with his cash for the church collection, there is no reason to think that she could not influence his point of view on issues facing the church. Though we have no direct evidence of women's behind the scenes maneuvering in the colonial Dutch Reformed church, it is instructive to consider the observation of a man who was active in New York City's Presbyterian church. Esther Burr related this ship captain's comment in her journal in 1754: "Capt. Bryant says they have four Popes in Newyork, women popes, and who do you think they be? Mrs Mercy, and Mrs Hazzard—Mrs Breese and Miss Nancy Smith—Mrs Breese is pope jone he says."[20] One cannot rule out the possibility that Dutch Reformed women, particularly those married to men who served on the consistory, similarly contrived to control the direction of church affairs.

A woman's most important role was to nurture the faith of those in the household who were dependent on her—her children, servants, and slaves. Though a mother's primary concern was to instill religious values in her own children, the responsibility for seeing to the spiritual welfare of all those who labored for the family also fell to a sizeable number of Dutch women, not just the privileged few. How seriously the mistress of a household took her religious duties toward servants and slaves is a subject in urgent need of investigation in view of the heavy involvement of Dutch Americans in slaveholding.[21] Judith Stuyvesant, the wife of New Netherland's Director-General, Peter Stuyvesant, evidently cared enough about the spiritual condition of the slaves on the family's Bouwery to see that the slave children were baptized. In 1664, Peter Stuyvesant arranged to sell some of the family's slaves and ship them to Curacao. A number of the baptized children were unwittingly included in the shipment. Judith Stuyvesant urged their recall, but it was too late. The baptized children had been lost in the abyss of that slave entrepot. The Dutch West India Company's Vice-Director on Curacao lamely apologized to Peter Stuyvesant: "[A] serious mistake...has

20. Carol F. Karlsen and Laurie Crumpacker, eds., *The Journal of Esther Edwards Burr 1754-1757* (New Haven and London, 1984), p. 74.
21. Recent scholarship on maid servants in the seventeenth-century Netherlands suggests the complexity of the relationship between mistresses and servants. See Marybeth Carlson, "A Trojan horse of worldliness? Maid servants in the burgher household in Rotterdam at the end of the seventeenth century," and Rudolf Dekker, "Maid Servants in the Dutch Republic: sources and comparative perspectives" in Els Kloek, Nicole Teeuwen, Marijke Huisman, eds., *Women of the Golden Age: An international debate on women in seventeenth-century Holland, England and Italy* (Hilversum 1994), pp. 87-96; 97-101.

been committed here in the sale of your Slaves; especially of the little Children, since with great forethought on the part of Madam Stuyvesant...they were presented at the baptismal Font. If we had the least knowledge of the fact, the mistake would not have occurred."[22]

Whatever their attitude toward servants and slaves, Dutch women felt strongly about the religious upbringing of their children. Particulars are lacking, but it is not hard to imagine Dutch Reformed mothers reading the Bible with their children, pointing to the scriptural tiles that decorated the hearth and repeating favorite Bible stories to the young ones, or drilling older youngsters in the lessons of the Heidelberg Catechism.[23] Mothers may have been the ones who insisted that their children be sent to the catechism classes conducted by ministers and schoolteachers. Nor did a mother's concern for the spiritual state of her offspring cease as the child edged toward maturity. Indeed, it might have intensified, given the temptations youths faced in the world.

In the correspondence between Jeremias van Rensselaer, the young heir to Rensselaerswijck, and his widowed mother Anna, in Amsterdam, we have a rare glimpse of the way in which religion entered the mother-son relationship. Though Jeremias was already in his twenties when she wrote these letters urging him to live up to religious precepts, Anna was undoubtedly dispensing advice of the same nature she had given her children throughout their lives. "Above all, fear the Lord God and keep Him constantly before your eyes and pray fervently that His Holy Spirit may guide you in truth. Go diligently to church and practice God's Holy Word, as thereby you may save your soul."[24]

22. "Vice Director Beck to Peter Stuyvesant. Curacao...the 15 November...1664," E.B. O'Callaghan, ed., *Voyages of the Slavers St. John and Arms of Amsterdam, 1659, 1663: Together with Additional Papers illustrative of the Slave Trade under the Dutch* (Albany, 1867), pp. 226-227.
23. According to Ruth Piwonka, "Dutch Bible illustrations and numerous religious subjects depicted on hearth tiles reinforced [biblical] instruction." Ruth Piwonka, "Recovering the Lost Ark: The Dutch Graphic Tradition in the Hudson Valley," in Nancy Anne McClure Zeller, ed., *A Beautiful and Fruitful Place: Selected Rensselaerswijk Seminar Papers* (Albany, 1991), p. 29. In the colonial Dutch Reformed church, children sat with their mothers. De Jong, *The Dutch Reformed Church in the American Colonies*, p. 137.
24. "Anna van Rensselaer to Jeremias van Rensselaer, Amsterdam, December 26, 1654, A.J.F. van Laer, transl. and ed., *Correspondence of Jeremias van Rensselaer 1651-1674* (Albany, 1932), p. 15.

Anna van Rensselaer felt no compunction about lecturing her adult son concerning right conduct: "always shun the company of light [women] of whom New Netherland is full, and guard yourself against drinking, which is the root of all evil. In short, I admonish you, as Paul the Apostle did Timothy, to exercise yourself in godliness, to give attendance to the reading of God's word and to watch yourself."[25] After learning that he was having financial problems, she advised him to scrutinize his own behavior: "perhaps, you are not serving God as you should. I understand from your brother that he has urged you several times to become a member of God's church, but that he has not been able to induce you to do so, because you wish to have a freer rein and to indulge in greater dissipation in this corrupt world, which grieves me exceedingly."[26]

Jeremias responded to his mother's indictment by affirming his religious faith. On June 8, 1660, he wrote her, "I therefore joined [the church] last year and made my confession of faith, so that I now also take communion at the Lord's table, in remembrance of Him." Moreover, he had resolved "to sing some psalms" during the long winter evenings. "I have learned to sing nearly all of them by myself, except a few, which I am still busy learning. I therefore beg you also to have Cornelis de Key again make me a psalter to fit these golden clasps, one of the thinnest and most oblong kind, to carry in the pocket."[27] He also requested his mother to obtain a rhymed psalter for him.

Jeremias's determination to live a godly life was confirmed by his choice of a bride. When he wrote his mother on August 19, 1662, announcing his marriage to Maria van Cortlandt, he hurried to assure her of the pious character of his new wife. "To put your mind at ease I shall only say that I thank the good Lord for His mercy in granting me such a good partner..., to live together so calmly and peacefully with a wife who has always led a good moral life and feared the Lord God is the best thing I could wish for here on earth."[28] He had chosen a wife in the mold of his mother, thereby

25. "Anna van Rensselaer to Jeremias van Rensselaer, Amsterdam, December 5, 1656," van Laer, *Correspondence of Jeremias van Rensselaer*, p. 37.
26. "Anna van Rensselaer to Jeremias van Rensselaer, Amsterdam, February 19, 1659," van Laer, *Correspondence of Jeremias van Rensselaer*, p. 131.
27. "Jeremias van Rensselaer to Anna van Rensselaer, [June 8, 1660]," van Laer, *Correspondence of Jeremias van Rensselaer*, pp. 230-231.
28. "Jeremias van Rensselaer to Anna van Rensselaer, In the Colony of Rensselaerswyck, August 19, 1662," van Laer, *Correspondence of Jeremias van Rensselaer*, pp. 300-301.

endorsing the critical role women played in sustaining religious values in the family. But women's religious life extended beyond the household.

Women proclaimed their faith publicly by going to church every Sabbath day and by joining the Dutch Reformed church. Becoming a church member was not automatic or inevitable, but a volitional act involving mastering the Heidelberg Catechism and confessing one's faith. Women attached a great deal of significance to their decision to join the church, since religion was the only arena in which a colonial woman could make an independent choice.

One might argue that electing to become a member of the Dutch Reformed church was really an empty choice, since most Dutch colonial women enjoyed no other viable options regarding church membership. Many dwelt in settlements where there were no other denominations, and those who lived in towns with more than one church were limited in their choices by the fact that the only language they knew was Dutch, and therefore they could not understand the sermons in another church. This argument overlooks the fact that one always had a choice between attending the Reformed church and becoming a communicant. In the Netherlands, because so many people who availed themselves of Reformed preaching and ritual acts failed to make the commitment to the Reformed church, a special term was invented for them—adherent.[29] The distinction between communicants and adherents persisted in New Netherland. Shortly after the surrender of the colony to the English in 1664, Domine Samuel Drisius informed the Amsterdam classis that he intended to stay on in New York: "We could not separate ourselves from our congregation and hearers, but consider it our duty to remain with them for some time yet, that they may not scatter and run wild."[30] The implication is that hearers were not members of the congregation, that is communicants.

Dutch women tended to join the Reformed church at an early age, a fact which suggests both the lasting imprint of their religious education and the resoluteness of their faith. In 1698, Dominie Selyns extolled the accomplishments of his female catechism students in New York City. "The

29.`A. Th. van Deursen, *Plain Lives in a Golden Age: Popular Culture, Religion and Society in Seventeenth-Century Holland* (Cambridge, 1991), p.262.
30. "The Rev. Samuel Drisius to the Classis of Amsterdam, Manhattan, September 15, 1664," J. Franklin Jameson, ed., *Narratives of New Netherland 1609-1664* (New York, 1967; originally published 1909), p. 415.

girls although fewer in number, had learned and recited more in proportion
than the boys."[31] Evidence assembled on the age at which women joined the
New York City church shows that a majority joined before the age of twenty
and more than three-quarters joined before marriage.[32] Women were
involved in church life in other ways. They had their banns published in
church and were married by the minister. Their children were presented for
baptism there. Judging from two references Jeremias van Rensselaer made
to his wife Maria being "churched" after giving birth to a child, Dutch
Reformed women also went through this ritual of purification, which has
ancient roots.[33] Considerable evidence exists that churching was practiced
in the contemporary Church of England, but it remains to be shown how
widespread this ritual was in the colonial Dutch Reformed church.[34]
Women frequently stood as godmothers or baptismal sponsors for the
children of relatives and friends. This duty seems not to have been taken
lightly. Margareta Selyns, the widow of Dominie Selyns, bequeathed to "all
the children whereof I have been Godmother, the sum of L6 5s, and they
are to produce a certificate thereof out of the Church Registry."[35]

   Women also contributed to church collections regularly and, on occasion,
made special gifts or bequests to the Dutch Reformed church. Once, when
Maria van Rensselaer was seeking to frame her plea for a particular piece of
property in the most powerful terms, she stated, "I only want it for a stiver

31. Edward T. Corwin, ed., *Ecclesiastical Records of the State of New York*. 7 vols.
    (Albany, 1901-16), vol. 2, p. 1235.
32. Joyce D. Goodfriend, "Dutch Women in Colonial New York," paper delivered at
    the American Society for Ethnohistory meeting, 1981. For data on the women in
    the Tappan Dutch Reformed Church, see Firth Haring Fabend, *A Dutch Family
    in the Middle Colonies, 1660-1800* (New Brunswick, 1991), p. 149.
33. "Jeremias van Rensselaer to Anna van Rensselaer, April 24, 1664;" "Jeremias van
    Renssealer to Oloff Stevensen van Cortlandt, [Water]vliet, January [5] /15,
    [1671];" van Laer, *Correspondence of Jeremias van Rensselaer,* pp. 349, 433. On
    churching in New Amsterdam, see Esther Singleton, *Dutch New York* (New
    York, 1909), p. 248.
34. On churching in England, see Keith Thomas, *Religion and the Decline of Magic*
    (New York, 1971), pp. 38-39; 59-61; and William Coster, "Purity, Profanity, and
    Puritanism: The Churching of Women, 1500-1700," in Sheils and Wood, *Women
    in the Church*, pp. 377-387.
35. Will of Margareta Selyns, 1711, *Collections of the New-York Historical Society*
    (1893), pp. 115-116. On godparentage among the colonial Dutch, see Edward H.
    Tebbenhoff, "Tacit Rules and Hidden Family Structures: Naming Practices and
    Godparentage in Schenectady, New York, 1680-1800," *Journal of Social History*,
    18 (1985): 567-585.

on Sundays for the poor."[36] Maria's sister, Catharina, the widow of Frederick
Philipse, in her 1730 will, bequeathed "a large silver beaker, on which my
name is engraven and a damask table cloth...with a long table, In trust for
the congregation of the Dutch church...at Phillipsburgh."[37] The records of
the First Dutch Reformed Church of Breuckelen reveal that in 1684, Maria
Baddia had presented the church with "a silver cup for the administration
of the Lord's Supper."[38]

But the most important information to be gleaned from church records
is that women joined the church in large numbers. Evidence assembled
from congregations in New York City, Schenectady, and Tappan, New York,
suggests that colonial Dutch Reformed churches exhibited patterns of
female numerical dominance similar to those of congregational churches in
New England and elsewhere.[39] Ascertaining the relative proportion of
females and males in other Dutch congregations at different points in time
in the seventeenth and eighteenth centuries will provide the requisite data
for testing the applicability of the "feminization" thesis to the colonial Dutch
Reformed church.[40] The large scale commitment of women to the Dutch
Reformed church is already a certainty, however.

Documenting the fact that women were the mainstay of many
Dutch Reformed congregations should cause us to think critically about the
possible influence women exerted on church affairs, even though they were
barred from official roles in church governance. Because women were
denied formal channels through which to make their opinions known, we
should not conclude that they had no opinions on the issues confronting the
church or that they had no impact on their congregations. Laurel Ulrich, in

36. "Maria van Rensselaer to Richard van Rensselaer, November 12, 1684," van
Laer, *Correspondence of Maria van Rensselaer*, p. 171.
37. Will of Catharine Phillipse, 1730/1, *Collections of the New-York Historical
Society* (1894), pp. 21-22.
38. A.P.G. Jos van der Linde, transl. and ed., *Old First Dutch Reformed Church of
Brooklyn, New York. First Book of Records, 1660-1752* (Baltimore, 1983), p. 101.
39. Joyce D. Goodfriend, "The Social Dimensions of Congregational Life in Colonial
New York City," *William and Mary Quarterly*, 3rd Series, 46 (1989): 257-258, 276;
Edward Henry Tebbenhoff, "The Momentum of Tradition: Dutch Society and
Identity in Schenectady, 1660-1790, Ph.D. Dissertation, University of Minnesota,
1992, p. 248; Fabend, *A Dutch Family in the Middle Colonies*, pp. 146-153.
40. On the "feminization" thesis, see Richard Shiels, "The Feminization of American
Congregationalism, 1730-1835," *American Quarterly*, 33 (1981): 46-62; Patricia
U. Bonomi, *Under the Cope of Heaven: Religion, Society, and Politics in Colonial
America* (New York, 1986): 111-115.

a study of Congregational women in revolutionary New England, has reminded us that women's "characteristic forms of participation were indirect" and that "devout women...working around the edges of formal organization managed to evangelize their sisters and sometimes influence their ministers."[41]

Prohibited by custom from speaking out in public, Reformed women nevertheless were free to air their views to other women as they sat side by side in the section of the church designated for female worshipers or when they visited in each other's homes. We know that female members of other churches met together for religious purposes. In New England, Puritan women gathered in informal prayer groups and in Pennsylvania, Quaker women carried out the work of their denomination through distinctive organizational structures called women's meetings.[42] Toward the end of the colonial period, Methodist women were grouped together in all-female class meetings.[43]

Dutch Reformed women must have shared their thoughts and feelings in informal private conversations throughout the colonial period, but evidence of collective female activity is lacking before 1765. In that year, Archibald Laidlie, the first minister to preach in the English language in New York City, "organize[d] special meetings where women by themselves, and men and youths by themselves expound the Scriptures by turns, repeat prayers from memory, discuss questions of conscience, etc. All this is also done with closed doors."[44] Laidlie's all-female group was perceived as a dangerous innovation by his orthodox colleague, Lambertus De Ronde. But we can speculate that the new meeting was a source of great satisfaction to the women involved. Not only was this a forum in which they were not

41. Laurel Thatcher Ulrich, "'Daughters of Liberty': Religious Women in Revolutionary New England" in *Women in the Age of the American Revolution,* ed. Ronald Hoffman and Peter J. Albert (Charlottesville, Va., 1989), p. 223.
42. On female prayer groups in New England, see Charles E. Hambrick-Stowe, *The Practice of Piety: Puritan Devotional Disciplines in Seventeenth-Century New England* (Chapel Hill, 1982), pp. 140-141. On Quaker women's meetings, see Jean Soderlund, "Women's Authority in Pennsylvania and New Jersey Quaker Meetings, 1680-1760," *William and Mary Quarterly,* 3rd series, 44 (1987): 722-749.
43. For an example of a female class meeting of Black women in New York City c.1770-1771, see Frederick E. Maser, ed., "Discovery," *Methodist History,* 10 (1972): 57.
44. "Rev. Lambertus De Ronde to the Rev. John Kalkoen, New York, September 9, 1765," Corwin, *Ecclesiastical Records of the State of New York,* vol. 6, p. 4006.

deemed subordinate, but the minister was present to validate their religious ideas.

Another means existed for women to make known their views on religious matters—the petition. Petitions were a highly traditional and legitimate form of addressing authorities, and there are a number of examples of women petitioning the New York governor for redress of grievances. The earliest instance of a colonial Dutch Reformed church document signed by females I have located dates from the New York City congregation in the 1750s, but a search of local church records might very well turn up an earlier example.[45] This document, a 1754 petition urging the New York City church to hire a minister who could preach in English, was signed by eighty-seven individuals, including fourteen females.[46] Before declaring the independence of mind of these women, however, we must examine the relationship of the female to the male signatories. If it turns out that these women were mainly wives or relatives of the men, then one would have to consider the possibility that they were just echoing the views of their male kinfolk. Nevertheless, this does not diminish the significance of their signing the petition. Those who drafted the petition, as well as those who received it, clearly recognized the collective power of the women of the Reformed church.

The opinions of Reformed women on ecclesiastical questions were more likely to be taken into account when congregations were sharply divided on fundamental matters. Though not given an opportunity to express their sentiments publicly, women could be confident that their preferences would hold weight in church deliberations. In the extended conflict over the introduction of English preaching that polarized the New York City Reformed congregation, the female supporters of the Dutch party—the faction that opposed English preaching—were identified as relatives of the men who took this position. A document recounting the situation in the church in 1762 related that "Mr. Hardenbrook & his Party [the Dutch party]...were then pretty considerable for numbers, amounting in the whole to Eighty

---

45. In 1684, thirty-five women signed a petition to the consistory of the Reformed Church in Leiden in the Netherlands. De Baar, "'Let Your Women Keep Silence in the Churches,'" 397.
46. Alexander J. Wall, "The Controversy in the Dutch Church in New York Concerning Preaching in English, 1754-1768," *New-York Historical Society Quarterly*, 12 (1928): 39-58.

three men with the addition of their Wives and Daughters."[47] Family solidarity took precedence over any gender-related concerns in this case. But a time would come when Reformed women were willing to take a stance at odds with that of their husbands.

Let me suggest, finally, that women may have affected the course of development of the Dutch Reformed church in colonial America by bearing its message to the family and the community. Because women were frequently the sole representatives of their families in a congregation, it is not unlikely that they served as the conduit through which ministers conveyed Reformed teachings to members of the family who had strayed from the church. We can also speculate that the views of Dutch Reformed ministers on political issues were broadcast to the Dutch community largely through the agency of women. Elaine Forman Crane, in a study of Rhode Island women in the Revolutionary era, has raised the intriguing possibility that women were "chains of persuasion" in circulating the political ideas of Congregational ministers in the town of Newport.[48] At the least, women's function as vehicles of communication merits investigation in the context of Dutch Reformed church history.

As we incorporate women into the history of the colonial Dutch Reformed church, it is imperative that we conceive of women as historical actors. Though consigned to passive roles in church affairs, women were never mere spectators. They made choices, they acted on their beliefs, they inspired their families. Nor were they a monolithic group. Dutch Reformed women who lived in rural settings confronted different issues from those who lived in New York City or Albany. Those whose families acquired wealth and power had a different vantage point from those for whom everyday life was a struggle. Some resisted change, others welcomed innovation. The task that lies ahead of us as historians of religion is to refine our understanding of the experiences of Dutch Reformed women in the colonial era and to endow those experiences with the legitimacy they so richly deserve.

---

47. "Consistory of the Dutch Reformed Church of New York, Answer to the Remonstrance of July 6, 1767, New York, September 23, 1767," Corwin, ed., *Ecclesiastical Records of the State of New York*, vol. 6, p. 4105.
48. Elaine Forman Crane, "Religion and Rebellion: Women of Faith in the American War for Independence" in *Religion in a Revolutionary Age*, ed. Ronald Hoffman and Peter J. Albert (Charlottesville, Va., 1995), p. 84.

III
The Dealings of the Lord's Love With Dina van den Bergh[1]

Johan van de Bank

On the occasion of my delivery of some guest lectures in the New Brunswick Theological Seminary in February and March, 1993, on the Dutch minister and poet Jodocus van Lodenstein (1620-77), among others, Dr. J. David Muyskens drew my attention to a Dutch manuscript in the Gardner Sage Library of that seminary. As he said, this manuscript frequently mentions the name of Van Lodenstein. It appeared that the splendid library possesses not only a diary for the year 1747 in which this name occurs, but also notes for the year 1749 and a letter, all written by the same young Amsterdam lady, Dina van den Bergh (1725-1807), who by her marriage to an American candidate for the ministry, Johannes Frelinghuysen, had come to New Jersey. It also appeared that the neighboring Alexander Library of Rutgers University possesses rather damaged notes written in Dutch by the same Dina for the year 1746 and also a number of her letters, some in Dutch

---

1. The author has published a Dutch edition of the collected notes, diaries, and letters of Dina van den Bergh discussed in this essay: *De leiding van des Heeren liefde met Dina van den Bergh* (Houten, 1994).

originals, some also translated into English. With photocopies of the manuscripts in my suitcase I returned to the Netherlands, where to my great surprise I came across an article in the Documentatieblad Nadere Reformatie by F. A. van Lieburg about the Tienhoven minister Gerardus van Schuylenburg (1681-1770) which also mentioned the name of Dina van den Bergh.[2] Van Lieburg had traced Dina van den Bergh through a letter she had written to the Rev. Van Schuylenburg, but he had not succeeded in establishing her identity. As a matter of fact he could not suspect that her trail would lead to America!

In use of language, wording, and contents, this letter quoted by Van Lieburg is in complete accordance with the manuscripts found in New Brunswick, so that it may be concluded that we have to do with the same woman.

Further research established that in the Gardner Sage Library there is also an unpublished typed manuscript by William Demarest (1813-74), minister of the Dutch Reformed Church of Ramapo, New Jersey, which gives a translation of the diary of 1747 and also mentions something about the history of the manuscript.[3] Via Dina's daughter Mary Nela the manuscript was handed down in the family for years, until it finally found a place in the Gardner Sage Library. The documents in the possession of the Alexander Library form part of a large collection of papers belonging to the Hardenbergh family, to which Dina belonged through her second marriage.

In 1993 a translation of the notes for 1746 and 1749 together with the diary of 1747 appeared as no. 3 in the *Occasional Papers* series of the Historical Society of the Reformed Church in America. The translator, the Rev. Gerard van Dyke, based himself on Demarest's earlier translation and on a few letters.[4] Both Demarest and Van Dyke met with problems caused by a lack of knowledge of eighteenth-century Dutch and by difficult passages that they were apt to omit in their translations.

2. F. A. van Lieburg "Gerardus van Schuylenburg (1681-1770), een piëtistisch predikantenleven," *Documentatieblad Nadere Reformatie* 16/2 (1992), pp. 103-29.
3. William Demarest, "Memoir and Diary of Dinah Van Bergh, Wife and Relict, First of Rev. John Frelinghuysen and afterwards of Rev. Jacobus Rutsen Hardenbergh, D.D., by William Demarest, Pastor of the Dutch Reformed Church of Ramapo, Author and Translator, 1868-69," manuscript in the Gardner Sage Library.
4. *The Diary of Dinah Van Bergh*, trans. Gerard Van Dyke, introduction and notes by J. David Muyskens (Historical Society of the Reformed Church in America: New Brunswick, 1993).

Dina van den Bergh writes in the way in which she undoubtedly spoke, that is in scriptural language or the "language of Canaan" (Isa. 19:18), which was for a large part derived from the *Statenvertaling*, the Dutch authorized version of the Bible (1637). Knowing, understanding, and speaking this language was more than just a matter of mastering the words; it also meant sharing in the benefits that are set apart for the elect in this life — sharing, that is, in the true experience of the saints.[5] It is remarkable that although Dina does quote Holy Scripture, she does not cite it by authors or books. Her quotation of Scripture texts, Psalms, and poems is hardly ever literal, so that we may assume that she quotes from memory. Besides the Bible and the psalms in Dathenus' Dutch rhymed version, it is particularly Van Lodenstein's poems and hymns, and to a much lesser degree another hymnbook, *Een Nieuw Bundeltje Uitgekipte Geestelijke Gezangen*, that shape her way of expressing herself.

It is unknown whether there are any portraits of Dina van den Bergh. We will have to make do with a comment, recorded by Demarest, made by a certain Mrs. Hageman, who remembered Dina because she had met her in person, describing her as "of medium stature, in complexion rather dark, with dark hair and eyes, neat and plain in her dress, and attractive in manner, and that no one could avoid loving her, so kind and gentle in disposition as not to have trouble with anyone, as endearing in her intercourse".[6]

The Amsterdam Period

Short Biography

Hardly anything is known about the origins of Dina van den Bergh. Even her name, which does not occur in the baptismal register of the Dutch Reformed Church of Amsterdam, presents problems. In her notes and in signing letters in her "American period" she regularly used the initials D.V.B.: Dina Van Bergh. However, the notice of marriage, in which on February 21, 1750, her marriage to Johannes Frelinghuysen is announced, names "Dina van den Bergh."[7]

---

5. C. van de Ketterij, *De weg in woorden* (Assen, 1972), p. 14.
6. William Henry Steel Demarest, "Dinah Van Berg," paper read before the Ulster County Historical Society, June 5, 1939, at Kingston, N.Y., p. 25. (Manuscript in the Gardner Sage Library.)
7. Municipal Record Office, Amsterdam, DTB 593, p. 189.

On the basis of her notes, her diary, and her extant letters, it is possible to sketch a short biography of this woman.

According to the tradition known in New Jersey, she was presumably born at Amsterdam on February 10, 1725, daughter of a well-to-do Amsterdam merchant, "Louis" Van Bergh, who had earned his fortune in the Dutch East Indies trade.[8] The same tradition states that the fourteen-year-old Dina protested against the card-playing of her father and his friends and that she succeeded in having it stopped.[9] Perhaps her own words that "even in the midst of my youth I was taken from the midst of an evil world while so marvellously and graciously led by God," refer to this event. In this, a resemblance is to be noted to other biographies from those days, from which it appears that most of the central persons described in them had no pietist fathers or mothers or at least do not mention them.[10]

Her account of Johannes Frelinghuysen's proposal of marriage states that in the period before February 1, 1742, she had lived through very anxious days. Five years later, in 1747, Dina wrote in her diary that at that time, on February 1, 1742, "her soul was set free." It is for this reason that eight years after this event she suggested in a letter to her betrothed Johannes that he set apart this day when "the Lord broke my bonds, and set me at liberty, and saved me from the deep darkness I was in" as a day of commemoration.

As a seventeen-year-old girl Dina was stirred by "a sweet desire to be allowed to do something on earth for the Lord" and the Lord "appeared [to her]" telling her that he would bring her to a people whose language she did not know. In 1749, the year of Frelinghuysen's proposal, she remembered that at one time the Lord had said to her that "He had work for her to do on earth" and that this would be made possible by means of a marriage.

A letter, unknown in America but published twice in the Netherlands, to the Rev. Van Schuylenburg at Tienhoven, dated September 22, 1744—Dina was nineteen at the time—indicates not only that she had been paralyzed for a period of about two years, but also that the Lord had saved and cured her by means of a miracle.[11] After her illness she was able to go

---

8. Demarest, "Dinah Van Berg," p. 10.
9. Demarest, "Dinah Van Berg," p. 5.
10. F. A. van Lieburg, *Levens van vromen. Gereformeerd piëtisme in de achttiende eeuw* (Kampen, 1991), pp. 39-40.
11. "Brief van Jufvrouw Dina Van Den Bergh van Amsterdam aan Ds. Schuijlenburg," in *de Christelijke verzamelaar door en voor het volk* 5 (1855): 275-79, and: R. van Masijk, *Wonderlijke Genezing Ds. G. F. Schuylenburg, 22 September 1744* (Rotterdam, 1918).

to church on September 30 of the same year; the service was led by the Amsterdam minister Temmink with whom she had had a very special spiritual relationship, for in her notes he is called her "tenderly loved father in Christ."

Two Guides

In Dina's early years, two ministers exerted a great influence on her: Gerardus van Schuylenburg (1681-1770) and Johannes Temmink (1701-1768). We learn to know the Rev. Van Schuylenburg of Tienhoven to some extent from the introductions that he wrote, sometimes under the pseudonym of Christophilus Parrhesius, for publications such as a reprint of Van Lodenstein's *Beschouwinge Zions* (1718), the translation into Dutch of the Scottish diary of Elisabeth Wast,[12] a translated treatise by John Owen on the sabbath (1744),[13] a few collections of sermons by the Dutch lay-preacher Justus Vermeer from 1746 and 1749, and an introduction to the Dutch translation of a booklet by Jonathan Edwards about David Brainerd, the Scottish missionary among the Indians of New Jersey.[14] Van Schuylenburg was a Reformed-pietist minister, who with great earnestness stressed the experiential knowledge of the Word, of the Mediator Jesus Christ, and of regeneration through the Holy Spirit. Living according to the seventeenth century ideals of the Nadere Reformatie (the "further reformation"), he followed in the track of Van Lodenstein and Jacobus Koelman in expressing reservations about the Christian feast days, the formularies and collects (formal prayers), which soon earned him the name of "Koelmanist." Van Schuylenburg showed his fear of unregenerates using the Lord's Prayer, of having their children baptized without any reflection, and of their taking part in the Lord's Supper as a matter of course. He was a friend to (pietist) lay preachers, even welcoming them to his pulpit, and he promoted the

12. Elizabeth Wast, *Zoet en bitter, licht en duisternis, op den weg naar den hemel, tot haar eigen en anderer bestiering opgeteekend in den loop van haar verborgen leven met God* (Utrecht, 1729).
13. John Owen, *Oeffeningen aangaande de Naam, Oorspronk, Natuur, Gebruik en Standhouding van een Dag van Heilige Ruste, waarin de oorspronk des Sabbaths van de grondlegging der Wereld, de Moraliteit van het Vierde Gobod, nevens de verandering van den sevensten Dag ondersogt worden* (Utrecht, 1744). Translation of *Exercitations concerning the name* ..., etc. (London, 1671).
14. Jonathan Edwards, *Historiesch verhaal van het godvruchtig leven en den zaligen doodt van den Eerwaarden Heer David Brainerd* (Utrecht, 1756). Translation of *An Account of the Life of ... Mr. David Brainerd* (Boston, 1749).

conventicles (the "companies of the pious"). In his warnings he did not mince words. It is especially the followers of Cocceius, the Cocceians, who have to suffer: in sharp terms he disapproves of their preaching, which does not have a separating spirit and contains all kinds of allegories and strange exegeses.

Johannes Temmink, for his part, accepted a call to Amsterdam in 1740, where he preached to full churches and was active till his death in 1768. We do not know how Dina came to know him personally, but it is clear that there existed a spiritual bond between her and this minister. Not much is known about Temmink. His colleague and friend, the Rev. Boskoop, described him as a man who "maintained the old proven truth, whatever wind of doctrine sprang up."[15] In his words, Temmink did not swerve "a hair's breadth" from the fundamental dogmas of the Holy Scriptures, "expressed in our Forms of Unity which are based on the Word of God." The pious, humble, sincere, and diligent Temmink was a serious and peaceful man. He regretted the differences among his local colleagues, differences which he "neither cherished nor stimulated, but rather wanted to be diminished, if not stamped out completely." Also from the accounts of his sermons that Dina gives us, we learn to know him as an experientially minded, orthodox, and irenic minister, who cannot easily be placed in some "faction" — in short a figure clearly different from his colleague in Tienhoven. Temmink's strength must have been in his pastoral care and his preaching. His sermons were not published during his lifetime in spite of insistent demand. After his death a few collections of homilies appeared, of which the exegesis of Jesus Christ's prayer in John 17 in the form of twenty-three sermons has been reprinted several times.[16]

Church Services and Conventicles

Dina van den Bergh reports on the services she attended in Amsterdam, down to the minutest details; the sermons are briefly reproduced, sometimes

15. Johannes Boskoop, *De opstandinge der Regtveerdige, s'Heeren Gunstgenooten voorgehouden in een Lykreden over Jesaja XXVI. v. 19. Ter Nagedagtenis van den Wel Eerwaarden en Godtzaligen Heere Johan Temmink, Wemm. Fil.* (Amsterdam, 1768).
16. Johannes Temmink, *Het Hogepriesterlyk Gebed van Christus of Verklaring over het zeventiende Capittel van het Euangelium van Johannes in XXIII Leerredenen, met een voorreden verrykt door Johannes Boskoop, des Overledens Amptgenoot* (Amsterdam, 1769). The library of the Vrije Universiteit in Amsterdam owns many manuscripts containing sermons of Temmink during the period of 1725-68.

even with their subdivision into "points." She has gone to church to get "food for her soul," and it is remarkable that she never expresses a negative opinion of these services. Among the names of the ministers that she mentions are followers of both Voetius and Cocceius and also opponents as well as supporters of the Moravian Von Zinzendorf. One gets the impression that Dina did not occupy herself with the theological differences of denominations within the Dutch Reformed church, but that she felt at home where, according to her, the Word was preached in a scripturally justified and experiential way.

The preparation (mostly on Saturday afternoon) for and the celebration of the Lord's Supper appear to have been decisive moments in her life. But she describes many other spiritual experiences as well — at home "in my seclusion," or "in my quiet time" and also during the services, in the prayer meetings, regularly held on Tuesdays with her female friends, and during the "conventicles," the meetings meant for mutual edification, where lay-preachers occupied themselves with the explanation of a scriptural passage. Dina also attended the "societies of the pious." There — in contrast to the regular conventicles' spontaneous meetings — knowledge and experience came up for discussion in an intimate atmosphere in which those present could find answers to their personal questions on faith. Even the excursions in the country that Dina made with pious friends, or her extended visits to a country-seat were dominated by these spiritual questions. Everything she experienced, including the outward beauty of nature or works of art, had to have an inner spiritual meaning.

Spiritual Life

In her writings Dina is humble and meek in the consciousness that she is miserable and unfaithful, that she has to struggle against a body of sin and that it is only through grace that the Lord has taken pity on her. Undoubtedly she has had to fight against a passionate character, as appears from the way she has treated a subordinate; she has "a bad and sinful temper," which she not only regrets afterwards, but for which above all she needs God's forgiveness. But also in later days, when the young candidate for the ministry, Johannes Frelinghuysen, proposes to her, she has to be saved from not simply refusing him in her impetuosity. This same quick temper also shows in her spiritual life, characterized by two phrases that occur again and again in her descriptions and indicate what she considers particularly sinful, namely "making reservations" and "running ahead of the Lord." "Making reservations" is in her diary the opposite of "surrendering to the Lord without any reservedness"; in spite of grace received she wishes to maintain something of her own. In her own words the "running ahead" is her main trouble. It is very difficult for her to await God's time, and in her sorrow about this she asks for "breaking and healing grace."

Thus she knows temptation from within, for which she accuses not only herself, but also the "enemy," the "evil one," who has tried to tempt her through wicked suggestions.[17] Again and again she longs "through grace to be made to live to the honor of Christ" and to serve the Lord truly. In this she finds her only support in the Word, in the Lord's promises. Besides this the Psalms, of course in Petrus Dathenus's rhymed version used at the time, Jodocus van Lodenstein's *Uytspanningen,* and *Een Nieuw Bundeltje Uitgekipte Geestelyke Gezange*n are the sources from which she continually draws.

The Making and Renewing of the Covenant

Several times, remarkably enough, one finds in Dina's literary inheritance mention of the personal covenant which is made with God and in God's presence, and which at decisive moments is repeated and renewed. The declaration is dated and signed with her own signature D.V.B. There may be some variation in phrasing, but as far as contents are concerned there is hardly any difference. Again and again everything can be traced back to the words of Isaiah 44:5: "One shall say, I am the Lord's; and another shall call himself by the name of Jacob; and another shall subscribe with his hand unto the Lord, and surname himself by the name of Israel." Five times we find Dina's initials under her testimony that she is "the Lord's servant"; she solemnly binds herself (again) to the Lord, who shows her that he is merciful. It becomes clear from the ten times when a covenant is made that the initiative does not lie with her, but with God himself.

This kind of personal covenant became current particularly in the latter half of the seventeenth century, and it is especially found among the Puritans in the writings of, among others, William Guthrie (1620-1661),[18] Thomas Boston (1676-1732), and the two Erskine brothers Ebenezer

17. Cf. Wilhelmus á Brakel, *Redelijke Godsdienst II* (Rotterdam, 1748), chapter 53, pp. 660-72.
18. William Guthry, *Des Christens Groot Interest, ofte Het Zalig Deel aan Christus, Getoetst en aangewesen wie het heeft, en hoe te verkrijgen. Met een Vertoog van de wijze hoe met God uytdruklijk een Verbond te maken* (Amsterdam, 1680). Translation of *The Christian's Great Interest*, etc. (London, 1667).

(1680-1754) and Ralph (1680-1752).[19] It is possible that Dina van den Bergh was led to it through a booklet by Elisabeth Wast, introduced in the Netherlands by the Rev. Van Schuylenburg, in which the principal person mentions the making of such a covenant, dated (August 11, 1694) and signed, on the occasion of the celebration of the Lord's Supper. But it may likewise be that some Amsterdam ministers conveyed the idea to her. Thus Dina reports that in the preface to a sermon on Psalm 25, which the Rev. Van Schelluinen delivered during the service of the Lord's Supper on April 30, 1747, he said: "It is in our heart that we make a covenant with the God of our fathers."

That such covenant-making occurred more widely becomes clear from a sermon by the New Jersey minister Theodorus Jacobus Frelinghuysen (the father of the Johannes who was later to marry Dina), which was published in Amsterdam in 1736. In this sermon on Joshua 24:22, also preached on the occasion of the Lord's Supper, this originally Dutch minister speaks of making a "personal, or solemn Covenant, as it is practised in the Church of Scotland."[20]

Weakness and Illness

Dina's notes show us that she was not physically very strong. From her letter to the Rev. Van Schuylenburg we may conclude that as a young girl she suffered from some kind of infantile paralysis, of which she was cured through a miracle of the Lord. But this physical weakness and illness are often mentioned afterward as well. She suffered from heavy fits of fever and it sometimes looked as if she were going to die. During her stay at Utrecht in 1747 her situation was to become extremely critical. She traveled to Utrecht by tow-boat with a friend, September 8, 1747, to stay there with "friends." In the Sunday services in the Utrecht churches as well in the meetings with the "friends," she experienced with joy that the Lord was with her. In spite of all this she believed that there were "trials" ahead, and this appears to have been true. A severe fit of fever brought her to the brink of

---

19. C. Graafland, *Van Calvijn tot Comrie. Oorsprong en ontwikkeling van de leer van het verbond in het Gereformeerd Protestantisme*, 3 and 4 (Zoetermeer, 1994), p. 310ff.

20. *Een Bundelken Leer-Redenen uit het Oude en Nieuwen Testament. Uitgesprooken door Theod: Jacob: Frilinghuisen, Bedienaar des H. Evangeliums in de Nederduitsche Gereformeerde Gemeyntens tot Raratans, in Nieuw-Jork, Eertyds Nieuw-Nederland* (Amsterdam, 1736), p. 151.

death. The Utrecht professor of medicine, Oosterdijk Schagt, who had been summoned to her aid, wanted her parents to be warned. Dina was ready to die and in this way to be released from "the body of sin": "there could be no more joyful news to me than that I should die, for I am reconciled to God, I step with Jesus into eternity." But this did not appear to be God's design; she heard the words: "You shall still enter through much tribulation, your work is not done." For a long time the fever persisted, and only gradually did her condition improve. On Friday, September 29, the physican in charge informed her that she would have to be nursed as a hothouse plant. Then things took an unexpected turn: she even managed to stand up and to walk about. The same evening she and the emotionally affected friends praised God's miracles and faithfulness in their prayers and by singing "some stanzas from the rhymed version of Psalm 118." On the next day, October 1, 1747— "the very day when three years before, after being wonderfully restored by God, I went to church" so Dina writes—she went to church and heard the Utrecht minister, who delivered a very applicable sermon and remembered her in his intercessory prayers.

The Political Situation

The notes made by Dina are, as we have noticed, first and foremost of a spiritual nature, but this does not mean that she closed her eyes to the circumstances of her country at the time. On the contrary, her account of 1747 in particular shows us the political situation of those days. The Netherlands were in danger of being overrun by France, which in 1744 had declared war on England and Austria. The French government had informed the government at the Hague that the Southern (Austrian) Provinces of the Netherlands could not remain safe. On April 17, 1747, it announced that the territory of the Dutch Republic would also be occupied. On the same day French troops invaded Holland. This resulted in a revolt in the Netherlands. In Zeeland, the first province to revolt, William IV was proclaimed stadtholder; and on May 2, 1747, the same proclamation was made at the town hall in Dina's hometown of Amsterdam. The entry into the town of the new stadtholder on May 11, Ascension day (!), and the merry-making that went with it, are approvingly described by Dina. All the same she was not, as so many others were, an Orangist as such. There was a deeper reason for her approval, for, as she writes: "I was aware of the wholehearted love I had for his Highness, ever since and in particular when I had become a subject of Christ." To her, Stadtholder William IV was "a second Gideon," called by the Lord to liberate the Netherlands, albeit with a restriction: "I was, at the same time, conscious of the desire to be preserved from placing our dependence in men instead of in God."

Dina probably also expressed her love of the House of Orange in poems: there is mention of a poem of thirty-eight stanzas and another of thirty-nine stanzas, dedicated to the prince and the princess of Orange-Nassau. The present whereabouts of the two poems, however, are unknown.[21]

Is there then in Dina's notes a notion of a reformed nation, based upon the idea that God has made a covenant with the Netherlands? Or is it rather a matter of "a second Israel," which does not so much refer to the nation as to the church? Whoever considers the many times that Dina van den Bergh speaks of Sion in her notes and her diary will arrive at the conclusion that both possibilities are present, but that in most cases "Sion" and "our country" are mentioned as two separate entities side by side.[22]

Marriage

It is conspicuous that Dina "experienced a strong desire to be made useful for immortal souls" and "to be allowed to do something for the Lord." She knows that the Lord has given her his promises at an early age already, for he will "bring me into a certain way or ways" in which his promises will be realized. But this will only become clear in the long run. When the Lord tells her that she will not remain "without child," her first thought is that she will "gain a spiritual seed."

It is in this light that we should view her description of the proposal of marriage that Johannes Frelinghuysen made to her in 1749. Already in 1747, during her stay at Utrecht, she had come to know, through "a providential direction of the Lord," this prospective minister, who had come to the Netherlands to be approved by the classis of Amsterdam to receive calls to the ministry in America.[23] When he came to visit Dina in Amsterdam, she initially thought that it was a farewell visit. But this candidate for the ministry — the son of Theodorus Jacobus Frelinghuysen (1692-1747), minister at

21. Theodore W. Welles, *Ancestral Tablets from Colonial Days to the Present* (Paterson, N.J., 1893).
22. Cf. C. Huisman, *Neerlands Israël* (Dordrecht, 1983) and: R. Bisschop, *Sions Vorst en volk* (Veenendaal, 1993).
23. *Boekzaal der geleerde Weereld* (1749), p. 715.

Raritan, who had left the Netherlands for America in 1719[24] — to Dina's astonishment proposed to her.

In spite of God's promises in the past and clear indications in her secret spiritual communion with him in the present, Dina put her "sweet security," her desire "to please the Lord without the attachment of marriage," above a marriage. Is this a matter of "piety of the single state"? In Reformed pietism this seems to have been a rare occurrence. A clear example is a certain Geesje Pamans (1727-1821), a contemporary of Dina, who in her autobiography, published in 1775, says that the intercourse with a man pales into insignificance beside "the spiritual bond of marriage with Christ, the fairest of sons of men." She hopes — as did Dina before she really understood God's promises — that through her, children will be born in Sion and that she may be a glad mother of many spiritual children.[25]

As for Dina: the prospect of a voyage across a dangerous sea, a future in a foreign country far from her parents and little sister, was at first an insurmountable obstacle to the young Amsterdam woman. Her father declared himself against the marriage without further reason, saying he would rather see her die than consent to a marriage. Her sister was very upset and her mother, who knew that the Lord had "prepared" her, was very afraid.

Johannes Frelinghuysen, however, persisted; and others lent their support, or at least dropped their opposition. Dina received the advice of one of "our reverend teachers"—perhaps the Rev. Temmink?—to accept the proposal, though he could not convince her. Dina tried to hide behind her parents, but they, too, finally held the view that if this matter was of God, they would not be able to stop it.

Ultimately Dina accepted the proposal and became engaged to Johannes. Even then, she appears at first to have hoped for a cancellation. She proposed twice to postpone to marriage—first for three years, and then for two—on the understanding that Johannes would return to America in the meantime. But Johannes refused to leave the Netherlands without her. The engagement seems to have caused her other anxieties as well. In a letter of

24. J. R. Tanis, *Dutch Calvinistic Pietism in the Middle Colonies. A Study in the Life and Theology of Theodorus Jacobus Frelinghuysen* (The Hague, 1967).
25. Geesje Pamans, *Egt verhaal van geestelijke bevindingen, uit een sterken gemoedsaandrang om te vertellen wat de Heere aan de ziele gedaan heeft, met geen ander oogmerk, dan tot ere van God, en stigtinge van den evenmensch. Uitgegeven naar Bentheimsche kerkenordre. Door Geesjen Pamans, lidmaat der gereformeerde kerke te Nienhuis, in de graafschap Bentheim* (Zwolle, 1775).

January 31, 1750 Dina mentions a note that she has received from the Rev. Van Schuylenburg of Tienhoven and that has brought her into a state of great confusion. Apparently there has been some gossip. With great emphasis she reports that she wants to be faithful to her husband-to-be, even if there are people who do not approve of this marriage.

The published notice of the marriage incidentally provides new evidence of the direct connection of Dina's adviser Van Schuylenburg to the Americans: it announces that on February 20, 1750, the bride, living in Amsterdam, will marry the minister who has been called to the church of Raritan on May 8, 1749, and who, at that moment, lives at Tienhoven! We can infer that Johannes was well acquainted with Van Schuylenburg. The inference finds support in the foreword Van Shuylenburg would write in 1755 to the Dutch translation of Jonathan Edwards's biography of David Brainerd (1718-1747), "Reverend Teacher of a Congregation of Christian Indians at New Jersey." There the Tienhoven minister commends to his readers' prayers the "remains of the Dutch Church in New York and surroundings (earlier called the New Netherlands)," and adds: "Since 1720 a powerful door has been opened there during the ministry of Theod. Jac. Frilinghuysen [sic] senior, who (besides several Presbyterian ministers) has been used for the rebuilding of the dilapidated walls of Sion and whose two remaining sons still work there fruitfully, together with other ministers, also those of the Scottish Church, which brothers, at least some of them, are in much danger of the enemies in these days."[26] Van Schuylenburg has surely heard of the activities of the father through his son, when the latter was a student and inhabitant of Tienhoven; and now even five years after Johannes Frelinghuysen's return to America he appears to be informed about the present state of affairs.

The approaching marriage was announced three times, both at Tienhoven and at Amsterdam. The names of Johannes and Dina are not to be found in the marriage register of Tienhoven, but they do occur in the marriage book of the New Church of Amsterdam, where it is written that on Monday, March 9, 1750, at 2:30 p.m. their marriage was blessed by the Rev. Temmink.

The American Period

The passage

Dina's fear came true: the passage to America across the "astonishing large sea" was far from easy. An American tradition reports that through

26. Edwards, Foreword.

terrible gales the ship sprang a leak and threatened to capsize; the pumps were not equal to their task and the captain warned passengers and crew that there was no longer any hope of salvation. Dina calmly sat on a chair that had been fastened to the mast, and prayed. During her prayer the water stopped flowing into the hold, the pumps began to manage their work, and the ship was saved. Later on it would appear that a swordfish had come to fill up the gap in the hull and in this way had closed the leak. The chair that Dina had sat in was called the "Ebenezer chair" from this day forward, and she used it during the rest of her life.[27]

Johannes and Dina Frelinghuysen-van den Bergh

On August 3, 1750, Johannes Frelinghuysen preached his first sermon in Raritan on the words from Psalm 45:16: "Instead of thy fathers shall be their children." From the little we know of him it may be assumed that he indeed continued in his now-deceased father's line. Thus, because his father's closest colleague G. H. Dorsius had returned to the Netherlands in 1748, he took it on himself to train young men for the ministry in the beautiful parsonage at Raritan (the present Somerville), for which his father-in-law had had the bricks transported. In this "kitchen seminary," as his opponents called it mockingly, they received their education. Frelinghuysen had to struggle against the "Anabaptists" and the "Pelagian English," as well as against colleagues who resisted the "true piety of the heart" and against ignorance.[28] With the example of his two brothers in view, he pled with the classis of Amsterdam to spare his brother Hen(d)ricus the dangerous voyage to Amsterdam to be ordained there, but the classis thought that he could not be allowed this.

In the four happy years that were granted to Johannes Frelinghuysen in Raritan with his wife Dina, they had two children, Frederick, born April 13, 1753, and Eva, born September 5, 1754. But then he fell ill and died on his way to a meeting of the Coetus (a body of both orthodox and pietistic ministers) in Long Island in September 1754.

Widow

Thus Dina was left behind with her two children in foreign New Jersey, far from her relatives in Amsterdam. From her two letters to her brother-

27. Welles, pp. 129-30.
28. Randall Balmer, *A Perfect Babel of Confusion* (New York, 1989), p. 135.

in-law Hen(d)ricus, her great sorrow becomes evident. In them she struggles with the question of God's guidance in her life but decides she may faithfully trust in the Lord. What else could she do now but return to the Netherlands? Therefore she has tried to sell Johannes's library, though there does not appear to be much interest in it. Her hope is set on either Hen(d)ricus, who has to be ordained in Holland, or on her brother-in-law Theodorus, who intends to leave for the Netherlands to collect funds for a training college for ministers. Theodorus, however, is hesitating to undertake the voyage on account of the imminent war between England and France, which will not only be fought in Europe, but also on the American continent.

In the period of delay something completely unexpected happened: a former student of her husband's, Jacobus Rutsen Hardenbergh (1736-1790), proposed to her. Dina, eleven years his senior, did not know of anything to say but, "My child, what are you thinking about?" Yet she accepted his repeated proposal, for she saw that a marriage with this prospective minister might be the way in which the Lord would fulfill his past promises that he "has work for her to do."

The Rev. and Mrs. Hardenbergh

Well over a year and a half after Johannes Frelinghuysen's death, Jacobus Rutsen Hardenbergh and Dina van den Bergh were married in Raritan. The date was March 18, 1756. Jacobus continued his theological study, and the married couple together with the two children from Dina's first marriage were accommodated at Rozendaal, the estate of the Hardenbergh family. In 1758 the Coetus granted Jacobus permission to preach, and he was called to the ministry in the church which before him had been served by Johannes Frelinghuysen and which now consisted of the settlements of Raritan, Bedminster, North Branch (the present Readington), Neshanic, and Millstone (the present Harlingen). Thus the family moved into the parsonage that at one time had been built for Johannes and Dina. About Dina in those days little more is known than that the members of the church actually made much of Mrs. Hardenbergh and that on Sunday afternoons, she was in the habit of discussing the sermon delivered by her husband with the churchgoers who stayed over between the services.[29] In 1757, on July 25, Dina gave birth to a pair of twins, Maria and Laura; afterwards Johannes (April 2, 1759) and Mary Nela (December 17, 1760) were born in the parsonage of Raritan.

29. Welles, p. 131.

The Hardenbergh family increased in the ensuing years; after a daughter Dina was born (September 7, 1762), mother Dina gave birth to a son, Jacob Rutsen (April 27, 1763), who, however, died some three months later. Afterwards Rachel (November 29, 1765), Jacob Rutsen (June 19, 1768), and Lewis (May 14, 1771) were born.

Jacobus Hardenbergh, with others, continued to fight for the Dutch Reformed Church to have a college of its own. It must have been a satisfaction to him that in 1766 and in 1770 permission was given by King George III to found such a college. In 1771 New Brunswick was chosen as its seat, in part hoping to attract students of the German Reformed Church in Pennsylvania through a favorable location. There was no official association with the Dutch Reformed Church, except for the stipulation that the president of the college—which would bear the name of Queen's College, the present Rutgers University—was to be a member. With the consent of the classis of Amsterdam a new form of organization was introduced in the church itself: for the church as a whole a "General Body" was created, subdivided into five geographically arranged "Particular Bodies," remarkable names, which in 1784, after the War of Independence, were changed to "synod" and "classes." Hardenbergh held the presidency of the synod in 1775, 1780, 1783, and 1786.

During the prelude to the War of Independence (1775-1783), as well as during its course, Hardenbergh was fully involved in civil affairs as a member of the General Assembly of the state of New Jersey. There was even a premium on his head; therefore, he slept in his parsonage with a loaded rifle under his bed. In this period the minister and his wife made friends with General Washington and his wife; for two winters the general made his headquarters in the Wallace farm, diagonally opposite the parsonage of Raritan. The Hardenbergh couple narrowly escaped the English troops, who set fire to the church of Raritan and looted the parsonage.[30]

Dina's son from her first marriage also took part in the War of Independence. In the beginning Frederick Frelinghuysen had studied theology, but ultimately he chose a military and political career. He later

---

30. Cf. James Tanis, "The Dutch Reformed Clergy and the American Revolution," in *Wegen en gestalten in het Gereformeerd Protestantisme, Een bundel studies over de geschiedenis van het Gereformeerd Protestantisme, aangeboden aan Prof. Dr. S. van der Linde*, ed. W. Balke (Amsterdam, 1976), pp. 235-56.

represented New Jersey in Congress and was appointed Major General by President Washington.[31]

In 1781 Jacobus Hardenbergh was called to the ministry at Marbletown, Rochester, and Wawarsing in Ulster County, New York, the region where he had spent his youth. Dina and Jacobus were accommodated at Rozendaal. For Dina this meant that she now lived in the vicinity of her daughter Eva, who had meanwhile married the army officer Casper van Nostrand. In Rozendaal, too, the relationship with Martha and George Washington—his headquarters was now in nearby Newburgh—was maintained. Their stay at the family estate came to an end in 1785 when the nearly fifty-year-old Jacobus was called to the ministry of the First Reformed Church in New Brunswick and at the same time was appointed president of Queen's College. Dina, who was then sixty, aided him as much as she could in his pastoral work in New Brunswick. She visited the sick, took care of the poor, and called on those who were concerned about their spiritual state. She also resumed her habit of talking with those who stayed over between the Sunday services.

The Hardenberghs' stay at New Brunswick was a blessed period. The number of members increased under his preaching and pastorate. His health, however, suffered much under the strain. When he died for sheer loss of strength November 2, 1790, he was fifty-four years old. For the second time Dina stood at the grave of her husband.

Mother in Israel

After her husband's death, Dina lived for a short period with her youngest son, Lewis, who had inherited the family estate of Rozendaal, and afterward with her son John in Raritan; and then she moved into the house of her son Jacob Rutsen in New Brunswick.

In the letters that have been preserved from these years —unfortunately few in number — she appears first and foremost as loving mother, who is worried about the temporal well-being and eternal salvation of her children and grandchildren. How joyful she is when she is allowed to hear good of them, especially when this good reaches beyond temporary welfare! Besides

---

31. Cf. Emily Frelinghuysen McFarland and Ross Armstrong McFarland, *The Frelinghuysen Family in New Jersey 1720-1970* (Cambridge, Mass., 1970), pp. 25-33.

this she does not cease praying for them, admonishing them and showing them the way to eternal life.

She describes her spiritual experiences in the same way she did in the years 1746 to 1750 in the Netherlands. Use of word and language have hardly changed. Only here and there do we come across words and phrases that have been corrupted when taken over from English. She has obviously stuck to Van Lodenstein and the other poets who are so often quoted in her earlier notes!

According to the tradition known in New Jersey, Dina was in contact with various ministers, and encouraged them, but never hesitated to reprimand them when this appeared to be necessary.[32] Together with the minister's wife, Mrs. Condict, and one Sarah Van Doren, she gathered children around her to teach them the Scriptures — the first step towards a Sunday school, which was to come into being in New Brunswick in 1799.[33]

Dina, who had been involved for years in the training of ministers, could not refrain from writing a letter to the Rev. John H. Livingston, when in the 1790s an attempt was made to combine the latter's professorship, to which he had been elected by the synod of the Dutch Reformed Church, with the presidency of Queen's College. In this letter she urges him to accept this call. Her exertion may have had a delayed result, for in 1810 Livingston did accept an appointment as president of Queen's College. Thereby the Theological Seminary of the Dutch Reformed Church, which because of its connection with the minister-teachers had led a wandering existence since 1784, found a permanent residence in New Brunswick.

A letter of 1803 to Dina's daughter Rachel is her last letter known to us, a last testimony of the ancestress of the Frelinghuysen and Hardenbergh families in North America. In it she testifies to the hope that is in her: "The Lord remembered me with foretastes of heaven's glory and of a rest that finally remains, where pain and sorrow will be no more and where we will be given eternal joy in the presence of God."

On March 26, 1807, Dina Hardenbergh-van den Bergh died at the age of eighty-one at New Brunswick. On her tombstone in the churchyard of the First Reformed Church is written:

> "This monument is erected to the memory of Dina Hardenbergh,
> relict of the Rev. J. R. Hardenbergh, D.D., S.T.D.

32. Demarest, "Memoir and Diary," pp. 56-58.
33. Cf. J. David Muyskens, *The Town Clock Church: History of the First Reformed Church, New Brunswick, New Jersey* (New Brunswick, 1991).

Of high attainments here in grace,
now resting in glory, died the 26th day
of March, 1807, aged 81 years.
Tell how she climbed the everlasting hills,
Surveying all the realms above;
Borne on a strong-winged faith, and on
The fiery wheels of an immortal love."

IV
The Dutch Women
in Two Cultures:
Looking for
the Questions

John W. Beardslee III

The two cultures of my title are Dutch and English, which will have to be further qualified as we go along. As for the concluding clause, "Looking for the Questions," I am not going to go very much beyond raising questions and reviewing some materials that perhaps bear on the answers, but I shall risk some tentative conclusions.

According to the *Christian Intelligencer*, the 1877 annual meeting of the Woman's Board of Foreign Missions (WBFM) opened with the reading of Scripture by a clergyman, prayer by another clergyman, the reading of the president's report, which had been prepared by the president, Mrs. Duryea, by a third clergyman. Then came the presentation of the treasurer's report. The reporter did not tell us who presented it. Then another clergyman introduced the first speaker, the Rev. Gerard Waterbury Scudder, of New Brunswick Seminary, class of 1855, a missionary to India.[1]

---

1. *Christian Intelligencer* 48/20 (May 17, 1877): 8. Although Mrs. Duryea is identified by the *Intelligencer* as president of the WBFM at the time, the organization's published reports identify her as corresponding secretary.

Scudder began his address by remarking that a meeting of this character, which he described as women assembled for the elevation of their own sex, was possible only in a Christian land. This was in the 1870s; now, on the eve of the twenty-first century, we face a very different world. Scudder, Duryea, and the others there assembled would have found it impossible to believe many things that we have witnessed, among them that sovereign Hindu and Muslim nations would exist and count women among their leading political figures. Scudder's observation represents a deep insight into the social reality of the time in which he spoke. That reality has been approached in this volume from another point of view, which has uncovered much of the Christian past that needs to be overcome. But the viewpoint from which Scudder saw his own time remains one without which we cannot understand our past or our journey. That is to say, rather than the disabilities of women he turns our attention to their privileges, even in 1877, in a "European" Christian country. Our specific concern now is two related western European cultures, those of England and the Netherlands, and their possible influence on that small portion of America, where if anywhere, the influence of Dutch culture ought to be visible.

In recent work, Martha Shattuck has shared with us her researches in the history of Albany that demonstrate some distinctive features of Dutch law and custom that were quite different from the English. Dutch law gave women a measurably greater amount of legal and economic freedom with consequently more opportunity for taking the initiative in society.[2] Her findings confirm the conclusions of Sherry Penney and Roberta Willinken published twenty years ago, and those of other researchers.[3] The relationships of this situation to church life are the subject of the present investigation. I have characterized it as the search for the proper questions.

The first question, on which many others depend, is, "Was this freedom in economic and legal affairs reflected in the life of the church?" This question is hardly worth asking, and I am ready to reply in the negative. Material in the history of women in the Reformed Church in America, as

2. Martha Shattuck, paper presented to the Standing Seminar in Reformed Church History, New Brunswick Seminary, February, 1994. See Shattuck, "A Civil Society: Court and Community in Beverwijck, New Netherland, 1652-1664" (Ph.D. diss., Boston University, 1993).
3. Sherrey Penney and Roberta Willinken, "Dutch Women in Colonial Albany: Liberation and Retreat." *de Halve Maen: Quarterly Magazine of the Dutch Colonial Period in America* 52/1 (1977):9-10,14; 52/2 (1977):7-8,15.

one capable scholar told me and others have been finding out, is elusive. Using a methodology that I have suggested to others, I have become deeply aware of the frustrations involved in its application to this matter. But certainly the comparison of official documents, constitutions, forms of government, and the records as regards the admission of women to church office gives little evidence to suggest that "Dutch freedom," if present, significantly influenced the course of events in the official circles of the denomination. And this, I suggest, is nowhere more the case than in those areas where Dutch influence in modern times has been the strongest.

Reading of church periodicals has brought to my attention interesting and poignant matters, many of which I once planned to share in this essay and a few I will. They mainly reinforced the impression that Dutch law and the social custom did not turn the church's attention toward women in any direction other than that taken by the English.

We now ask the next question, "Why was this the case?" We must immediately turn to a series of further questions. First, how "Dutch" was the Reformed Protestant Dutch Church and its predecessor in the North American dependencies of the Classis of Amsterdam? Then, what kind of Dutch were these Dutch men and Dutch women? We must then ask these questions over again regarding the immigrants of the nineteenth century. With regard to the eastern part of the church, the question of how Dutch it was must be answered, certainly for the entire period of national independence, by saying that a recognizable Dutch element was constantly becoming less and less a factor, in spite of a certain pride and inspiration drawn, I think, largely from a version of Dutch history that owes much to the Yankee historian, John Lathrop Motley, and the pleasant irony of the satires of Washington Irving. The Dutch theological degree of John Henry Livingston, the church's first theological professor, may have helped establish his prestige at a critical moment. But during his lifetime American-educated Presbyterians were holding important positions in the church. His successor as professor of theology and Rutgers College president, Philip Milledoller, had no Dutch background, either ethnic or educational. At the same time, the use of the Dutch language was rapidly passing away. It continued to be spoken in homes in certain areas but was rapidly discontinued as a medium of worship and of church record-keeping. This was not a new development— in spite of the prevailing Dutch preaching during the colonial era.

To look back into the colonial period, the weight of history there had steadily been pushing the church away from a strictly Dutch heritage, and the stubbornness of the conservative opposition to some pressure from Amsterdam for union with Presbyterians in a college reveals an awareness of this among those who did regret it.[4] Use of English in business forced at least the men to become familiar with the language. Daily contact with the English population, use of English newspapers, if any were used, and subjection to English law all had their effect, as well. Adrian Leiby documented the influence of a Scots schoolmaster in the Dutch center of Hackensack and the impact of Princeton Presbyterians on the coetus clergy of New Jersey.[5] It is true that a few Scots people, like John Livingston's parents, became members of the Dutch church. And here and there, an "outsider" was really assimilated into the Dutch community. Leiby mentions an example.[6] But on the whole, the Dutch community was being influenced by the majority around it far more than it was influencing it.

As to how Dutch were the "Dutch" from the beginning, the Dutch colonists were ethnically an extremely mixed group. They included persons recently more or less assimilated, I think frequently less assimilated, speaking Dutch but willing to emigrate because they were not at home in the Netherlands. These included people from the French-speaking areas to the south whom we would now call Belgians, people from Switzerland and Germany, and an occasional refugee or adventurer from Poland or Scandinavia. There were also unassimilated foreigners among them. The first worship service in New Amsterdam was attended by many Flemings, that is, Belgians. The first two Dutch Reformed elders to be ordained in North America were men born in Germany, and so were many of the colonial clergy. After 1665, there was an influx of genuine French people, many of whom became part of the Dutch church. In 1710, a large group of Palatine Germans was settled along the upper Hudson and soon their settlements spread along the upper Mohawk Valleys. James Good, the Corwin of the German Reformed Church in North America, is the authority

---

4. See, e.g., Howard Hageman, *Two Centuries Plus: The Story of New Brunswick Seminary* (Grand Rapids, 1984), pp. 1-15.
5. Adrian C. Leiby, *The Revolutionary War in the Hackensack Valley: The Jersey Dutch and the Neutral Ground, 1775-1783* (New Brunswick, 1962), pp. 154-55.
6. Ibid., p. 93.

for the statement that in the later eighteenth century, one-third of the membership of the Dutch church was German.[7]

So much for comments of the Dutchness of the Dutch church even in colonial times. There would be ample opportunities for the dilution of Dutch customs and traditions. In the mixing of traditions, both Huguenot and German would undoubtedly have a place, but the tradition that could provide a coherent pattern for living in an English environment would be that of the English majority. The phrase "coherent pattern" suggests part of any answer to the next question that has been proposed. What kind of Dutch were these Dutch people? It is easy to forget that in many ways Dutch culture in the seventeenth century was fragmented. Behind the brilliant urban commercial culture lay provincial and local differences—dialects, social customs, degrees of economic development, religious differences, even, and sometimes especially, in Reformed churches. George L. Smith, in his book *Religion and Trade in New Netherland*, documents the religious pluralism that characterized seventeenth century Dutch cities, despite the efforts of the official church to make good its privileges. He also documents the various legal, extra legal, and illegal measures by which public toleration and public order were achieved in the Dutch golden age, and he thinks he can show a reflection of all these pluralistic forces in New Amsterdam.[8]

Under such conditions, differences within the Reformed church were inevitable. The myth of a solidly Calvinistic Netherlands was zealously cultivated by some in the Netherlands after the confused period of the French Revolution and Napoleonic occupations, as Gerrit ten Zythoff has shown us.[9] No doubt this myth influenced later generations of Dutch immigrants and also sympathetic members of the older Reformed Church in America. On the other hand, tribal memories of the old Dutch situation may have contributed to our ability to live together in spite of our obvious pluralism. It was pietism of largely Frisian origin, represented especially by two German-born clergymen, Freeman and Frelinghuysen, that first precipitated the great schism of the colonial period and eventually laid the

---

7. Cited by George Schnucker, "The German Element in the Reformed Church in America," in *Tercentennary Studies, Reformed Church in America*, ed. W.H.S. Demarest et al. (New York, 1928), p. 422.
8. George L. Smith, *Religion and Trade in New Netherland: Dutch Origins and American Development* (Ithaca, 1973), parts III and IV.
9. Gerrit J. ten Zythoff, *Sources of Secession: The Netherlands Hervormde Kerk on the Eve of the Dutch Immigration to the Midwest* (Grand Rapids, 1987).

denomination's principle source of unity. Christian life based on this pietism was very different from the Albany variety on which Shattuck, Penney, and Willinken based their work and was often incapable of appreciating its open-mindedness, diversity, or "worldliness."

In Albany, what Alice Kenney called "an urban variant of the Reformed faith" played a most important role.[10] It was a form of the Reformed faith very different from the rigid scholasticism of some of the other communities or the Frisian pietism or the new growing combination of pietism and scholasticism represented by theologians like Voetius. The Albany variant has at least social affiliations with that is sometimes called Cocceianism, that Reformed way of life that led socially prominent ladies to do their embroidery on Sunday afternoons in a room with windows open to the view from the street, as an advertisement of their freedom from the law. Add to this the fact that Albany held a peculiar position in the early years of the English colony. It was a stable, prosperous Dutch community, a fairly secure center for defensive and later for offensive military operations during a century of intermittent war with France. It becomes evident that the English, for a generation, had to pay attention to the feelings of these well-established fur trading burghers who had influence in the councils of the Six Nations and easy communication with Canada. Studies of the situation in Albany, in other words, may be misleading for the Dutch church and the Dutch communities as a whole. And even in Albany, the leading Dutch families soon ceased treating their daughters as people prepared for economic freedom. This change occurred early in the eighteenth century as English customs had their impact, as Penney and Willinkin documented through a study of the wills and the arrangements for female education.[11]

For the church as a whole, such hard evidence as I have found so far is not conclusive, but it does not lead me to abandon the view that Dutch women's "secular" privileges played little part in church life. It is interesting to learn that one of the two first comforters of the sick, the first ecclesiastical appointments in New Netherlands, was a man who had been illiterate at the time of his marriage and had married a literate woman. Literacy among Dutch women, to which Shattuck has referred, was not confined to the mercantile and property-owning class. This may give us a certain insight into

10. Alice B. Kenney, "Religious Artifacts of the Dutch Colonial Period," *de Halve Maen* 52/4 (1977-78): 1-2, 14, 16, 19.
11. Penney and Willinken, op.cit., p.15.

Amsterdam society. Research may lead to further insights into the colonial situation derived from the Netherlands, but tentative conclusions may stand for now.

It is also interesting to note that at a critical point in the American Revolution, Governor William Livingston of New Jersey made a special appeal to the Dutch women, saying that having been long accustomed to wearing the britches, they could now afford to give their wool petticoats to be made into blankets for the soldiers.[12] We have here a glimpse of the Dutch feminine fashions of the time and perhaps also a hint about the family and social standing of Jersey Dutch women, but we do not get away from the peculiar conditions of Albany because that is where William Livingston came from. He had been as a boy a member of the Dutch Reformed Church there and had undoubtedly formed lasting impressions about Dutch society. In the century and a half between the arrival of the comforters of the sick and Livingston's appeal, many Dutch women, at least in the church, seem to have achieved the ideal which Pericles held forth to the women of Athens: they are not spoken of, either for good or for ill, and their contributions, as with those of that comforter's wife, are inconspicuous. Frederick Philipse (Anglicized eventually as Philips) was twice married. Both of his wives receive a good deal of mention in the locally written histories of the Reformed Church of North Tarrytown, New York, partly, I think, because of the lack of other data. From a base in New York, Frederick became a great land owner and eventually, under English rule, about 1690, acquired the English title of Lord of the Manor and its privileges under New York English colonial law. His first wife, referred to as Lady Margaret, seems to fit a pattern roughly like that of some of the Dutch businesswomen of Albany. Associated with him in business deals, she also bought land for him. Her reported shipping activities may have made her (as well as her husband) one of those smugglers whose importance in our church has been pointed out by Daniel Meeter.[13] Her husband built (that is, he paid for) what is now called the Old Dutch Church of Sleepy Hollow (formely North Tarrytown, New York). Precisely what part his wife played in the actual life of the church

12. Leiby, pp. 143-44, quoting *Archives of the State of New Jersey*, second series, 1:532.
13. Daniel J. Meeter, "The 'North American Liturgy': A Critical Edition of the Liturgy of the Reformed Dutch Church in North America, 1793" (Ph.D. dissertation, Drew University, 1989), pp. 156-57.

as distinguished from the locally written eulogies is difficult to determine. Lord Frederick's second wife, Lady Catherine, is placed at the head of a list of church members dated 1714 as "first of all the Right Honorable, Blessed, Very wise, Foreseeing Lady Catherine Philips, widow of Lord Frederick Philips of blessed memory who did in this locality, in a most praiseworthy manner, further the service of God."[14] If the less-wealthy members of the church were blessed, wise, and foreseeing, the fact is not deemed worthy of record. Whatever special place these two women had in the history of the church may be attributed largely to their family status, the status of their husband as lord of the manor under English law. There may be room for further study of Dutch women in New Amsterdam and New York, especially in commercial circles.

Similar conclusions may be reached concerning the Beekman women in the history of the church of Rhinebeck, New York.[15] Like the Philipses, this family, which was allied by marriage to the Livingstons, had manorial privileges and in the mid-eighteenth century enjoyed the privileges of seats of honor in the church. At Phillipsburg (North Tarrytown/Sleepy Hollow) the seats of honor faced the congregation under a red silk canopy, an ideal position for imitating Sir Roger De Coverly, counting the congregation to see which of their tennents were absent and generally supervising the lower orders. Margaret Beekman inherited her father's extensive property simply because there was no male heir—a system which the English upper classes well understood—and the pious historian who chronicled her greatness emphasized, after the manner of our older pietism, especially her role as the mother of great sons. The Philips and Beekman women, like Wesley's supporter the Countess of Huntingdon, were, insofar as they contributed to the church, persons outside its structure—primarily members of a privileged class and secondarily privileged women within that class. But the privileges and manners of a privileged class do, in time, influence affairs in a widening circle.

In short, evidence of any carryover of Dutch women's privileges into the Dutch Reformed Church in this country as a significant part of its heritage

14. David Cole, "Historical Address," in *Three Hundredth Anniversary of the Old Dutch Church of Sleepy Hollow* (Tarrytown, 1898), pp. 114, 122, 126; *The First Record Book of the Old Dutch Church of Sleepy Hollow* (Yonkers, 1901), 8 (entry dated 1715).
15. Frank De Witt Blanchard, "Rheinbeck," in *Tercentenary Studies*, pp. 320-323.

and tradition has not been found. Reasons are not hard to find, and I have already given some. The brevity of Dutch rule, lack of any unified and unifying Dutch tradition, the constant pressure of English custom and law, the mixed ethnic traditions, and the growth of a biblicist-pietistic doctrine opposed to empowering women—all these factors were working. The urban Reformed faith of Albany was perhaps a form of what today we call liberalism. Voetus might have said "lax." I would prefer to call it Christian humanism, but that implies an intellectual sophistication foreign to the seventeenth century frontier life. It was not in harmony with the stricter forms of pietism that flourished particularly in New Jersey, and that came to be felt as the true Christian heritage of the denomination.

An interesting piece of evidence can be found in Kenny's findings that paintings of biblical scenes, which were frowned upon in certain circles (apparently, they were too much like icons), were common in Albany and were found elsewhere in the Hudson Valley, but not in New Jersey.[16] It had been claimed that opposition to the theater (a mark of pietism) on the part of Theodore Frelinghuysen, Jr., who was a product of New Jersey pietism, caused him a great deal of trouble and heart-searching and possibly discouragement, in Albany.[17] His pietistic moralism was invading the region of Dutch women's empowerment and causing tensions as it acquired power, as his father's convictions had done.

As a sort of appendix to this first section, I comment on a brief statement by Gerald De Jong. He declares that in the 1760s there seem to have been "Dutch" women in Albany who carried on evangelization among the native Americans who made seasonal visits to the area.[18] His authority is a nineteenth century book that admittedly must be used with critical caution.[19] Martha Shattuck has advised against reliance on it.[20] The author, a woman of marked romantic tendency and imagination, had lived in Albany for a few years as a little girl, the daughter of a British army officer. The book represents memories written down many years later, in an environment

16. Kenney, op.cit., p. 16.
17. Robert S. Alexander, *Albany's First Church and Its Role in the Growth of the City* (Albany, 1988), p. 126.
18. Gerald F. De Jong, *The Dutch Reformed Church in the American Colonies* (Grand Rapids, 1978), p. 160.
19. Anne MacVicar Grant, *Memoirs of an American Lady with Sketches and Scenery As They Existed Previous to the Revolution* (New York, 1846), pp. 65, 69-70.
20. In correspondence with the author.

influenced by Sir Walter Scott. It is obvious that she exaggerates the success of these missionary efforts, and other problems with her book are easy to find. But if one thinks in terms of the sort of things that might have impressed a little girl's mind and memory, some probabilities do emerge. She mentions that the Dutch women were confined to domestic activity, which agrees with the findings of Shattuck, Penney, and Willinken for these years. She describes the native Americans as, in effect (not her words) peddlers, dealing with the women at the kitchen door, a point that probably would have impressed the little girl. On the large scale, her description of Yankees corresponds to the reported attitudes of upper-class Dutch and of regular army officers, which can be found in other sources.

Hers is the only known book by a woman on Albany at that time, and we have learned not to despise childhood memories for biographical purposes, which are a form of social history. Her description of relations between white people and "wandering" native Americans is similar to my grandmother's memories from mid-nineteenth century Iowa, except that Grandmother never mentioned Indian evangelization by the good Methodist women of her family.

In the absence of further data, one must not hasten to conclusions. I find only the barest hints of similar activities outside the home by other women of of the period. That evangelization through the Christian family was not unknown in eighteenth century American is indicated, for example, by Connecticut legislation requiring those who employed "Indian" servants to give them instruction in the English language and in the Christian faith.[21] But this legal requirement in a settled situation, corresponding to the common obligations to an apprentice, is quite different ffrom the voluntary activity among seasonal migrants reported by Mrs. Grant.

In spite of problems with the evidence, it is legitimate to ask whether these Albany Dutch women, deprived of their former secular empowerment but not altogether ignorant of it, may have transferred some of the energy that the church structure had not yet welcomed into the field of Christian mission, so that they form one small thread in the many that eventually were woven into woman's missionary societies.

When we turn to the later large-scale Dutch immigration of the 1840s and later, new features appear. To return to our first question, "How Dutch are

21. George L. Clark, *A History of Connecticut: Its People and Institutions* (New York and London, 1914), p. 51.

we?", this movement, which gave the denomination its large midwestern section, was unquestionably Dutch. It determined the quality of our denomination's Midwest, although it must be remembered that in the Midwest there were the so-called nonimmigrant churches and there were important nonimmigrant leaders in Hope College and Western Seminary: windows of American life into the immigrant community. There were also groups of German-speaking East Frisians who became part of our midwestern church. But its overall Dutch character for a century and even now is undeniable. There were provincial and other differences, but the immigrant groups had a bond of unity not only in ethnicity and language but also in common adherence to a particular form of Reformed church life that very clearly defined it against those outside. It was based on experiences in the Netherlands quite different from those of the Dutch of the seventeenth century. One may mention the fruits of the eighteenth century Enlightenment, the French Revolution, the Napoleonic regime, and, under King William (once referred to in the *Christian Intelligencer* as the worst of the reigning sovereigns in Europe) union with Catholic Belgium, and resulting political adjustments. These and other features had produced, in a segment of the population of the Netherlands, a reaction based on the older Calvinistic pietism stiffened by an uncompromising adherence to certain scholastic forms of theology and a consciousness, historically oversimplified, of "Dutch" as "Calvinist."

The eastern church, in the first half of the nineteenth century, had been characterized by an extraordinary orthodoxy as was noted by Philip Schaff, an acute though rather unsympathetic observer,[22] and this undoubtedly helped in winning the allegiance of the new immigrants. This orthodoxy was leavened by a pietism out of which sprang the living bond of unity in the emerging denomination of two diverse parts separated by geography, and "shaped like a dumbbell," as someone said in General Synod.[23] There were genuine differences even where pietistic influences predominated. Pietism in the eastern sections had become revivalistic and had taken on specific American characteristics. The new immigrants were not originally revivalists. When revivalism appeared among them, it was evidence of

22. Philip Schaff, *America: A Sketch of Its Political, Social and Religious Character* (repr. Cambridge, Mass., 1961), p. 124.
23. According to my mother's vivid memory of a passionate address.

"Americanization." Tobacco was not an issue among the Dutch, although smoking by women became a major issue, contrary to the Dutch tradition of Albany as described by Shattuck. Total abstinence, when it appeared, is another mark of Americanization, and there were other differences.[24]

What is common to the two sections of the church, East and West, was a combination of biblicism, pietistic outlook, and scholastically oriented Calvinism, which, among other teachings, happened to take literally the prohibition on women speaking in church or having rule in the presence of men. This in a difficult period helped unite the church. Two bonds of unity developed: the foreign missionary movement and this mixed but effective piety. It was not until a new biblical hermeneutic emerged that any form of what we now call feminism could take place within the church except as a disruption. The Dutch tradition of women's empowerment, long forgotten in the eastern part of the church and never of ecclesiastical significance in it, was no part of the outlook of the new atypical Dutch immigrants who formed the backbone of the communities that gave new growth to the Reformed Church in America. Women's empowerment would have been part of that world they wanted to escape, if they thought of it at all.

Such forces as gave unity to the new diversity of the Reformed church, therefore, kept the new American movement for women's rights at arm's length from the church. Not until forms of theological thinking foreign to both sections were well established could a women's movement be part of its life.

But there were forces that paved the way for change. Advertisements in the *Christian Intelligencer* reminded readers that once in a while a woman did well in business—for example Lydia E. Pinkham. More important was that paper's interest in girls' education — a limited interest in many ways, slow in extending to higher education, but a very real interest. Advertisements for girls' schools, female academies or seminaries, appeared from the earliest issues. The first editor of the paper, C. D. Westbrook, was proprietor of one of these schools, and the woman in actual charge of his girls' school was the paper's first woman contributor, Amanda Buckley. Her writing was sentimental and home-centered, "appropriate for a woman," but integral to

24. Elton J. Bruins, *The Americanization of a Congregation*, 2nd ed. (Grand Rapids, MI: William B. Eerdmans Co., 1995), pp. 22-24, 25-27.

the paper.[25] It is to the advertisements of some of the other schools that I would turn particularly for indications of what persons with services to offer thought would appeal to readers of the *Christian Intelligencer*, which was still oriented towards the eastern churches in the 1840s and 50s. In addition to the conventional "polite" subjects, such as music, drawing, and French, facilities for education in the sciences often appear as special commendations of these girls' schools. Mention is made of collections of minerals and of scientific instruments that the pupils were to learn to use. And this is at the beginning of serious scientific education in secondary schools in the United States.

Over the century these notices become less frequent. Perhaps this was because of the growth and improvement of public schools, perhaps for other reasons. As we know from other sources, one of the common justifications of women's education at this period was that it made them better mothers, better able to educate their sons, and so on. Nevertheless, the church paper gave public approval to some real intellectual training for young women. There are articles of appreciation based on public ceremonies and receptions at the girls' schools. This approval of up-to-date female education represents the beginning of something greater, and as the number of educated women increased, questions as to the purpose of such education were bound to arise. It was an example of church participation in an American movement. Coeducation in the midwestern colleges later had a very similar effect, probably going far beyond what those who first introduced it expected.

A most important insight into the process is, however, the one hinted by brother Scudder in his address to the Women's Board of Foreign Missions in 1877. Whatever the failings of Christian patriarchy, women in European, and Christian, society enjoyed freedom denied their sisters in other countries. Women of respectable social status were not confined to women's quarters or to the home. Their feet were not bound. They were not burned on their husband's funeral pyres.

25. The following items are signed "Amanda B___": correspondence under heading "Miscellaneous," *Christian Intelligencer* 1/1 (August 7, 1830): 1; "Leaves of a Diary," ibid. 1/2 (August 14, 1830): 3; "Leaves of a Diary," ibid. 1/5 (September 4, 1830): 1. She writes as a resident of the village of "F___" — presumably Fishkill, where Westbrook had been pastor and had run a school prior to his removal to New York as editor. A notice in ibid. 1/5 of the opening in Harlem of a new school, "Harlem Institution," with Westbrook as its "superintendent and proprietor," identifies "Miss Amanda Buckley, Principal of Female Department" (p.3).

As a teacher of Old Testament at Central College, I may have startled students from time to time with my claim that there was one great charter of women's rights in the Old Testament—the passage in Amos that denounces the "cows of Bashan" (Amos 4:1). By holding women morally responsible, the prophet conferred full human status upon them. With all its faults, the Christian church and western society demanded moral responsibility of women. Church women responded. Through missionary societies and other avenues, they took responsibility for work that lay at hand, in Christian, and, if one will, in "womanly" ways, creating new opportunities as time went on. The dynamic worked within the faith. Secular traditions, whether Dutch, "Roman," English aristocratic, Enlightenment, or whatever, were secondary factors. At this stage, however, all conclusions are tentative.

V

Pious and Powerful:
The Evangelical Mother in Reformed Dutch Households, New York and New Jersey, 1826-1876

Firth Haring Fabend

In the nineteenth century, when evangelicalism and its products, moral reform and the benevolence movement, were transforming American society, the Reformed Dutch Church's influence over its adherents, particularly pious women, was never stronger.

Pious women in nineteenth-century evangelical households did not become so overnight. Their piety was the work of a lifetime of effort on behalf of their parents, their ministers and teachers, their extended families, their friends, the temper of the times. If they were affiliated with the Reformed Dutch Church, they had most likely been born into pious families and received from their earliest years a thorough grounding in the principles of their faith, both at home and at church. Many underwent powerful conversion experiences in their girlhood, taught in Sabbath schools as young women, and entered upon good works through an array of associations such as the American Sabbath Union, the Lord's Day Alliance, the Anti-Saloon League, and the ubiquitous Dorcas societies and Mite societies.

Piety infused even their social life. Diaries and letters of nineteenth-century Reformed church women from Albany to the Hackensack Valley to

66

the Raritan Valley, in Manhattan, in Brooklyn—in every area where the church flourished—document intensely active social lives centered around church-related activities. But even in secular pastimes, ranging from hayrides to parlor games, the most significant fact about the social life of women and men in the Dutch culture areas is that they mingled almost exclusively with other young people brought up in the same religious culture as themselves. In this way, common values, beliefs, mores, expectations, and customs were constantly reinforced in daily face-to-face contacts with the same people.

Concern for the girl child's spiritual welfare was manifested by family, clergy, and friends at every stage and turn in her life, and the details of the pious woman's spiritual journey, her conversion, her good works, the state of her soul at the hour of her death, and her role in bringing her family to the Lord were recounted in her funeral sermon and published in her obituary, especially if she had been the wife of a minister, or a beloved "mother in Israel," a minister's stalwart ally in the congregation. When Mary S. How, wife of the Reformed minister Samuel B. How, died in 1837, he baptized their fifteen-day-old child beside the mother's corpse, and in this central sacrament of the faith, their daughter Cornelia, aged fourteen, held the baby in her arms. Cornelia's role was a symbolic one that captured the centrality religion was meant to play and would play in her own life.[1]

Even more than her concern for her own salvation, the evangelical mother anguished over her children's spiritual welfare, and it is this particular aspect of her religious life I will focus on here. But first we must take a look at the term *evangelical* itself, which has changed in connotation since the nineteenth century. And we must look at the way evangelicals understood Heaven and Hell, concepts that today lack much of their nineteenth-century puissance.

"Nothing but the Bible"

Evangel is a word whose ancient Greek root means the bringing of good news. The good news the Four Evangels told was, of course, that God had

---

1. Both boys and girls received an intense indoctrination in the faith. See Firth Haring Fabend, "Suffer the Little Children: Evangelical Child-rearing in Reformed Dutch Households, New York and New Jersey, 1826-1876," *de Halve Maen*, vol. 68, no. 2, pp. 26-33. At this ceremony, where Cornelia held the baby, her brother Henry, twelve, had a role also, in holding the bowl of baptismal water. How Papers, Special Collections, Alexander Library, Rutgers University, New Brunswick, N.J., December 27, 1837. (Hereafter, references to the Special Collections at Rutgers will be cited as RUL.)

sent Jesus Christ to save humanity from sin. As the meaning of the word evolved, *evangelical* came to describe in nineteenth-century America those Protestant sects and denominations whose religion, as one preacher put it, "is the Bible, the whole Bible, and nothing but the Bible."[2]

By this standard, the Roman Catholic church, even though it preached Christ crucified and risen to redeem humanity, was not considered evangelical, because over the centuries it had introduced nonbiblical elements into its doctrine and practice. To be evangelical was to adhere precisely to what could be found in the Bible and to doctrines, confessions, standards, liturgies, and systems of church governance based upon it.

Denominations considered evangelical by this definition were the Congregational, Presbyterian, Baptist, Methodist, some branches of the Episcopal, and the Dutch Reformed. Among these the Reformed Protestant Dutch Church was the "little Benjamin"—in numbers the smallest, flourishing in 1826, when I begin this history, only in New York and New Jersey. Though the "little one," the Reformed Dutch Church considered itself the "purest in doctrine"—the one adhering most closely to biblical models and to the Bible-based confessions of faith, catechism, liturgy, polity, and doctrinal standards it had adopted at the Synod of Dort in 1618-1619.[3]

Some of these standards had shown signs of wear and tear in the two centuries since Dort, however, particularly the canons adopted at that synod. They declared that God had chosen the elect, and absolutely nothing one could do on earth could get him to heaven if he were not among those foreordained to go. The doctrines of total depravity, unconditional election, limited atonement, irresistible grace, and the perseverance of the saints did not suit the mood of Americans in the optimistic, self-reliant republic.

2. Robert Baird, "Religion in America" [1844], quoted in *The American Evangelicals, 1800-1900[:] An Anthology*, ed. William G. McLoughlin (Gloucester, Mass., 1976), p. 40. When John Pershing Luidens accused the Reformed Dutch Church of the eighteenth and nineteenth centuries as lacking an "evangelistic attitude," he was using twentieth-century connotations of the term: overtly enthusiastic, emotional, zealous, crusading, etc. Luidens, "The Americanization of the Dutch Reformed Church," diss. University of Oklahoma 1969, p. 368.
3. Even as early as the end of the seventeenth century, Reformed preaching in New York and New Jersey, as in the Netherlands, had begun to deemphasize the doctrines of predestination, election, and limited atonement and place emphasis on personal piety rather than strict orthodoxy. John W. Beardslee III, "Orthodoxy and Piety: Two Styles of Faith in the Colonial Period," in James W. Van Hoeven, ed., *Word and World: Reformed Theology in America* (Grand Rapids, 1986), p. 11.

Without ever officially disavowing them, the Reformed Dutch Church, at least in its progressive quarters, had by 1826 by and large come to tolerate the more moderate idea that God had given human beings free will and therefore they could and indeed must work to make themselves worthy of grace and salvation. By repenting their sins, keeping God's commandments, availing themselves of the sacraments, desiring grace, and diligently seeking the all-important conversion experience, human beings could hope to spend eternity in God's presence, rather than in Hell, the fearsome lake of never-ending fire.[4]

Heaven and Hell were not mere metaphorical concepts in the nineteenth century. They were very real places in the evangelical cosmology, territories

---

4. In 1793, when the first English translation of the *Constitution* of the Reformed Dutch Church was prepared under the direction of John H. Livingston (1746-1825), "The doctrines of Dort were [officially] maintained, but local ministers and consistories were left free to follow the leading of the Spirit of God," according to Reformed theologian Eugene Heideman, "Theology," in *Piety and Patriotism: Bicentennial Studies of the Reformed Church in America, 1776-1976,* ed. James W. Van Hoeven, (Grand Rapids, 1976), pp. 99, and 101-102. The preface to the *Constitution* contained a startling statement the significance of which no one at the time seems to have commented upon: "The unerring Word of God remaining the only standard of the Faith and Worship of his people, they [his people] can never incur the charge of presumption, in openly declaring what to them appears to be the mind and will of their Divine Lord and Savior." To some strict doctrinal conservatives within the church who later noticed it, this seemed to imply that it was permissible for Reformed persons to worship according to the dictates of their own conscience. In 1793, the notion that members of the Reformed church could not be accused of heresy by believing "what to them appeared to be" the revelation of God was a theological innovation, if not heresy itself.
   Livingston was prompted to incorporate this language into the *Constitution* in order to address the spirit of the age. He did not mean by it, although he was later accused of this, that what the correct Reformed church adherent believes is a matter of personal choice. Rather, Livingston was recognizing a growing willingness at this time on the part of many Protestants to accept differing understandings of, or to look for new insights into, Holy Scripture. God's revelation is ever the one fixed standard, but, he was implying, interpretations of that revelation continue to evolve. Although it was far from being an abdication of Dort, Livingston's concession to contemporary trends was nevertheless a momentous step forward on the part of the Reformed Dutch Church. Heideman has called it a "decisive American element" in Reformed theology, because it introduced tensions into the theology of Dort, "Theology," pp. 98-99. John W. Beardslee III, personal conversation, April 2, 1996, and personal correspondence, April 4, 1996. See also Firth Haring Fabend, "The Synod of Dort and the Persistence of Dutchness in Nineteenth-Century New York and New Jersey," *New York History,* LXXVII (July 1996), pp. 273-300.

whose geographical vividness was drawn for both children and adults in the sermonic literature, Sunday school curriculum material, and juvenilia of all evangelical denominations. The mind, wrote the Reformed minister Thomas Vermilye, "cannot fully comprehend [Heaven's] adorable perfections yet we know from the Scriptures that it is a place, not a condition." Among the legions of clergymen who described Hell, William C. Brownlee, another Reformed minister, was one of the most eloquent. Hell, he confidently assured his readers, was an immense and barren plain containing no speck of vegetation. Scathed by fire, it was inhabited by black-clothed multitudes with horror-stricken countenances, who under their black cloaks were a mass of blazing flames from their heads to the soles of their feet. It was from Hell that the evangelical mother was enjoined to save her children, and it was a heavy responsibility, for in an era when germs were unknown and antibiotics a century away, death was a frequent visitor to every household, and Hell was the certain destination of all but the saved—even little children.[5]

"A Nursery for Heaven"

The idea that Christ died for all, not just for the elect, was a blessed relief to the religious minded in the nineteenth century. But it also had the effect of putting enormous pressure on evangelical churches to persuade their adherents of the necessity to work toward their own salvation. As evangelical fervor gripped America, churches became aware that, in the daunting task of saving souls, they needed all the help they could get. For the Reformed Dutch Church in the 1820s this meant acknowledging that the limited resources of the denomination itself and the hard-working ministers it licensed were not sufficient to the challenge. It thus began at this time to establish Sunday schools, to join other evangelical churches in Sunday-school unions, and to participate in the publishing programs of the American Sunday School Union and the American Tract Society. By 1830 it was publishing its own weekly magazine for the laity, the *Christian Intelligencer*, a venture whose stated goal was to shape the minds and morals of every

5. Thomas Vermilye, "A Funeral Discourse Occasioned by the Death of Mrs. Cornelia Van Rensselaer...Delivered in the North Dutch Church, Albany, on Sabbath, the 1st September, 1844" (New York, 1844); William C. Brownlee, *Lights and Shadows of Christian Life: Designed for the Instruction of the Young* (New York, 1837), pp. 370-371.

member of the Reformed church. But above all, it was learning to enlist parents in the cause. And of all the sources the church brought to the struggle to save souls from Hell, the pious mother became the Reformed Dutch minister's strongest supporter.

From a practical standpoint, mothers were considered to be more important than fathers in the process of getting children saved, simply because mothers spent more time with their offspring. But there was also a theoretical basis for mother's role in the innovative ideas of the gifted Swiss educational reformer Johann Pestalozzi (1746-1827), who emphasized the importance of the mother in instilling love, confidence, and the desire to obey in her child. Evangelicals could not be content with such a secular grounding for their agendas, however, and a guide for mothers highly recommended by the Reformed clergy predictably resorted to the Bible to put things on a more theological footing: Because Eve, a woman, had been the first transgressor, "The world's redeeming influence...must come from a mother's lips. She who was first in the transgression must be yet the principal earthly instrument in the restoration...the great agent in bringing back our guilty race to duty and happiness....O mothers!," the author of this popular guide wrote, "reflect upon the power your Maker has placed in your hands....God has constituted you the guardians and the controllers of the human family."[6]

Other scriptural foundation was found for mother's role in the religious education of her family, some of it of a more positive nature. "By woman," wrote the "Parents and Children" column in the *Christian Intelligencer*, "came the apostasy of Adam, and by woman the recovery through Jesus. It was a woman that imbued the mind and formed the character of Moses....It was woman that led the choir....which went forth to celebrate...the overthrow of Pharaoh....It was not woman who denied her Lord at the palace of Caiaphas...."[7]

Fathers had a role to play, too, of course, but, "Woman is the most important sex," because, according to a view endorsed by the editors of the *Intelligencer*, she "forms our character, she watches by us in sickness, soothes us in distress, and cheers us in the melancholy of old age. Her rank

6. John S. C. Abbott, *The Mother at Home; or The Principles of Maternal Duty Familiarly Illustrated* (New York, 1833), pp. 160-61. Pestalozzi outlined his methods in the popular *How Gertrude Teaches Her Children* (1801). For his influence, see Kate Silber, *Pestalozzi: The Man and His Work*, 2nd ed., 1965.
7. The *Christian Intelligencer* (hereafter *CI*), July 11, 1850, p. 4.

determines that of the race. If she be highminded and virtuous, with a soul thirsting for that which is lofty, true and disinterested, so it is with the race. If she be light and vain, with her heart set only on trifles, fond only of pleasure—alas! for the community where she is so, it is ruined."[8]

Mothers were charged by the church with teaching their children the first step toward salvation: obedience. The importance of obedience in the religious culture of the evangelical era cannot be understated. Obedience was the key, the logic being that children who did not obey their parents would not obey God. And the child who did not obey God was surely destined to spend eternity in Hell. In special guides written for them, mothers were instructed that no act of disobedience was too small for concern. It was not a little thing to disobey a mother's command. After all, "The eating of an apple banished our first parents from paradise."[9] And mothers were told to expect more than a "languid and dilatory yielding to repeated threats….[It is not enough] that a child should yield to your arguments and persuasions. It is essential that he should submit to your authority" promptly and cheerfully.[10]

On the subject of child rearing, Reformed ministers preached and published many sermons, and the synod itself authorized the publication of tracts outlining the duties of parents—and the duties of children. Parental authority must be early and firmly established, uniformly maintained, and as pervasive as the "light of heaven" itself, prominent Reformed minister John Knox told his congregation in the Middle Dutch Church in New York in 1834.[11] Knox did not mince words: When children are "vile," it is parents who are to blame. Vile children are those who display temper, disobey, indulge "unholy gratifications," associate with wicked children, and neglect the Sabbath. Punishment was in order for children of this sort. "Let coertion [sic], when needed, not be weakly, and with mistaken fondness, withheld. Let control be positive….Let them be taught to fear sin, and to be under just restraint." Or, Knox warned, be prepared to suffer as Eli did: His sons died, Israel was invaded and defeated, the ark of God was captured by the Philistines, Eli collapsed and died, his daughter-in-law died in childbirth, eighty-five members of his grandson's family, not including women and

8. *CI*, February 28, 1835.
9. Abbott, ibid., p. 38.
10. Abbott, ibid., p. 25
11. John Knox, "Parental Responsibility and Parental Solicitude; two discourses, delivered in the Middle Dutch Church" (New York, 1834), p. 16.

children, were murdered by Saul, and one surviving family member was deposed from priestly office by Solomon and banished. And all because Eli "failed utterly in the exercise of due parental control."[12]

Attention to the child's salvation must be relentless. Parents must speak to their children about their salvation "in the house and by the way, rising up and lying down," Knox insisted. "Especially let Christian mothers devote themselves to this work," a tract published by the Reformed Dutch Church stressed. "Lead them daily to the cross. Teach them to pray. Take them with you and pray for them. Let them hear your earnest intercessions for them....Teach your little ones to sing the songs of Zion, and labor to make your dwelling a pure and peaceful abode, a school of Christian courtesy, the home of every social and spiritual grace."[13]

Conscientious mothers were expected to use guilt, fear, and anxiety as everyday weapons in the war of getting children saved. Children, mothers were told, should be made to feel that they have been bought with a price and that they must live as becomes the children of God: "Train them to the habit of secret prayer, to attendance on prayer meetings, to regularity at public worship, to reverence for the name of God and for his holy day. Train them to [have] respect for the aged, for ministers, elders, teachers, and all who are in office. Train them to a sacred regard for their own word; to punctuality and integrity...to habits of politeness and kindness...and to regular and systematic benevolence." And "observe that you are to train [them] thus,...not simply teach or advise them, but authoritatively to require them to form these habits....This will indeed demand pains, patience and prayer on your part," this tract acknowledged. "But, will you...neglect it? Dare you? Can you?"[14]

Ministers reflected tenderly on their training by their own mothers. Historically, from its origins, the Reformed Dutch Church had recommended daily family worship morning and evening and strict Sabbath observance, including attendance at morning and afternoon public services, as well as Sabbath evening worship at home. As the church expanded its efforts to save souls in the nineteenth century, family worship, particularly on Sunday evenings, took on special significance. Sabbath evenings, Reformed minister

12. Knox, ibid., pp. 8-17.
13. Knox, ibid, p. 16; and Board of Publication of the Reformed Dutch Church (hereafter RDC), *Tracts*, 2 vols. (New York, 1858), "Duties of Parents," *Tract No. 12*, vol. 1, p. 4.
14. RDC, *Tract No. 12*, pp. 2-3.

Isaac Ferris wrote, are "peculiarly fitted for gathering around us our beloved circle, and seeking their everlasting good." Sabbath evenings with his brothers and sisters around their mother's knee, reciting the catechism, reading scriptures, reporting on their reading and the public worship services of the day he recalled as the happiest evenings of his youth. To Ferris, there was "not a more interesting sight than that of a family…gathered around a beloved parent, and hearing from his or her lips the words of eternal life." Often, a glistening tear, a heaving breast will be evident as children apprehend the evil of sin and "personal unworthiness," he wrote. "Such a circle how truly a nursery for Heaven!"[15]

Home was sacred, and mother was its high priestess. In fact, by 1865, the tenth Commandment (Thou shalt not covet…) was viewed as "God's 'homestead law,'" in which he recognizes home "as a sacred spot…and source of every good affection."[16]

Although the popular guide already mentioned, *The Mother at Home*, published in 1833 by the American Tract Society, was written by a Congregational clergyman, it was often excerpted in the *Intelligencer*, and it was regularly advertised in this publication. It was the policy of the Tract Society to publish only works approved by all members of its board, and on its board always sat a Reformed Dutch clergyman. So we can assume that the advice *The Mother at Home* dispensed echoed from Reformed pulpits and in Reformed households throughout this period. Indeed, *The Mother at Home* is representative of the kind of "suitable mental aliment" read and recommended by all evangelical denominations for the mothers in their congregations.[17]

The Mother at Home was nothing if not specific in its advice. Mothers were encouraged not to supply children a reason for their every command. Rather, to "bring your child under perfect subjection….Sometimes give him your reasons; [sometimes] withhold them. But let him perfectly

15. Isaac Ferris, "Domestic Christian Education: A Sermon" (Albany, 1835), pp. 26-28.
16. *CI*, October 5, 1865, p. 157.
17. The same is true of the American Sunday School Union, whose board of directors included members of all the main branches of the evangelical Protestant churches and which published nothing without consent of at least three members of different denominations. Even one dissenting voice would halt the publication of any work considered. Edwin W. Rice, *The Sunday-School Movement and the American Sunday-School Union*, 2nd ed. (Philadelphia, 1917), p. 143.

understand that he is to do as he is bid," for without absolute, immediate, and cheerful obedience, "your family will present one continued scene of noise and confusion…[and] your heart will be broken by [your children's] future licentiousness or ingratitude." Mothers should never give commands they do not intend shall be obeyed, lest the child become used to discount her. Tell the child once and only once what you want her to do, and then punish her if she disobeys. The first rule of family government is to enforce obedience to every command in order to establish the principle that a mother's word is never to be disregarded.[18]

God had given mothers the power to obtain their children's prompt obedience, but mothers must start to do so when the children were very young. Even a fifteen-month-old child could be taught "by the serious tone of her mother's voice, and the sad expression of her countenance." If her helpless babe disobeyed her, the mother was advised "to cut off its sources of enjoyment, or inflict bodily pain, so steadily and so invariably that disobedience and suffering shall be indissolubly connected" in the child's mind. The too-tender mother who could not summon herself to deprive her baby of pleasure and to inflict pain when it was necessary must prepare for a broken heart and an old age of sorrow—when her dissolute sons and ungrateful daughters would remind her that in their infancy she might have checked their disobedient propensities. "And when at Judgment Day you meet your children and they say to you 'It was through your neglect of duty that we are banished from heaven and consigned to endless wo[e],' you must feel what no tongue can tell."[19]

To maintain her authority, mothers were cautioned against being too severe, however. A mother had to rule her children by striking a careful balance between making them fear her and making them love her. "Fear is a useful and a necessary principle in family government. God makes use of it in governing his creatures." But mothers who attempted to control children exclusively by this method would find that home would become an "irksome prison" instead of a happy retreat of peace and joy. In recommending *The Duty of Mothers* by E. N. Kirk, the *Intelligencer* printed an extract: "Would that mothers knew the virtue and power of a frown and a kiss, for with those instruments of terror and love, a child may be governed almost entirely before it can speak." Smiles were also a weapon in the arsenal: "Do

18. Abbott, *Mother at Home*, pp. 28, 37.
19. Abbott, ibid., pp. 38-40, 57.

you smile [at your children] sweetly, heavenly, joyfully—with Jesus in your soul? Well, smile on, keep smiling, day in, day out…[until your] little one smile[s] in return.…Mothers beloved,…who knows but those smiling sermons were the secret of secrets" of the mothers of Moses, Samuel, and Timothy? Mothers should be affectionate and mild. They should "sympathise with [their children] in their little sports" and gain their confidence by indulging their wants. Greet them with smiles, reward them with caresses, address them in tones of mildness and affection, govern by kindness, but when kindness fails, "punish as severely as necessary."[20]

If mothers must punish their children, they should do it in sorrow, not in anger. The "judicious" mother should first remove her disobedient or unruly child from the scene and tell him kindly but sorrowfully that she and God are most displeased with his conduct. Then she should put him to bed, kneel by his side, and ask God to forgive him. In the morning, when he agrees that he is sorry for his misdeeds, she should suggest that he ask for forgiveness, both from her and from God. "Thus, by judicious management, the desired object [obedience] is…perfectly attained, while the contest is avoided."[21] Mothers had to be manipulative, almost Machiavellian in the challenge of getting their children saved.

As for mothers themselves, they must at all times control their passions and never fly into a rage and beat a child. They must construct limits to their own power and never punish their children by exciting imaginary fears about ghosts and monsters, or by locking them up in cellars or dark closets, apparently a favorite chastisement of the day. And they must keep a careful eye on their domestic help. One three-year-old shut up by a maid for a few minutes in a dark closet went into a fit and remained for life an idiot, and "thousands upon thousands of human beings have been deprived of their senses" by such means, Abbott assured his readers.[22] The message to mothers was that in a well-governed Christian home, they, not their household help, must be in control of their families at all times.

The faults and errors of the evangelical mother included talking about her children in their presence, praising them, deceiving them, and continually finding fault with them. But her most egregious defect was not to be religious herself. "It is vain to hope you can fix your children's affections

20. Abbott, ibid., pp. 61-62; and *CI*, November 28, 1840, and March 31, 1870.
21. Abbott, ibid., pp. 61, 47-48.
22. Abbott, ibid., p. 109.

upon another world, while yours are fixed upon this," Abbott wrote. If a mother has not given her heart to God, she could be sure that she and her children would end in Hell. In "A Thought for Prayerless Mothers," a dying young man exclaims, "You are the cause of it, [mother]! I am just going into eternity...[and] black despair, and you are the cause of it," because she had allowed him to fish and hunt on the Sabbath. If a mother did not seek God for herself and her child, then through all eternity she must gaze upon the wreck of the child's immortal spirit "when both [mother and child] might have been reposing in heaven."[23]

Mothers were advised to take advantage of every occasion when their children might be particularly susceptible to religious discussions. If a little girl in the neighborhood dies, for instance, a mother might take her own daughter to the funeral: "As she looks upon the lifeless corpse of her companion...speak to her of the eternal world to which her friend has gone—of the judgment-seat...of the new scenes of joy or wo[e] she has entered...[and] tell her that she too soon must die; leave all her friends; [and] appear before Christ to be judged....There are few children who can resist such appeals." The "raging storm, the hour of sickness, the funeral procession, the tolling bell" all presented opportunities for pious mothers to lead their children's thoughts to God.[24]

It was important that heaven be presented in as attractive a manner as possible. It was a mother's privilege and duty to describe heaven to her children in such a way as to inspire them to want to go there. If your son has a thirst for knowledge, tell him that in heaven he shall understand all the wonders of God's works and comprehend all the machinery of nature. If your daughter loves music, "carry her thoughts away to companies of happy angels, with celestial harps and divine voices rolling their notes of joy through heaven's wide concave." Mothers must "present heaven to [their] children as...crowded with images of delight...till their hearts are warmed...[and they] listen with interest to how salvation is to be obtained." Dwell particularly on the Savior and his suffering. This will "awaken contrition and melt the heart....Your child will listen with tearful eye;...[and to] his tender mind will be conveyed an idea of God's kindness as nothing else can produce." It was quite common in this era for even very young children to have significant conversion experiences, and if their own

23. Abbott, ibid., pp. 113-116; and *CI*, "Parents and Children" column, May 8, 1845.
24. Abbott, ibid., pp. 123-125.

children did not show early evidence of piety, mothers were told that much of the blame was theirs.[25] In their letters and diaries, women expressed deep anxieties over children known or suspected not to have been converted.

A "different race of mothers"

Theoretically, the evangelical mother's dearest dream was that her son enter the ministry, but in fact it seemed that not enough of them did so. In his *Appeal to Mothers* published in 1844, Reformed Dutch missionary to India John Scudder excoriated parents for failing to dedicate their children to the promotion of the gospel. As a result, young men were shunning the ministry as a career. They "profess" the cross, but do not bear it, Scudder wrote. They pray "Thy kingdom come," but they refuse to make it come. "The sapling has grown into a tree, and every effort to bend it [now] is useless." And nothing will change, he prophesied, until the church is blessed with a "different race of mothers"—a race of mothers who will impress upon their sons, starting in infancy, their obligations to enter the ministry.[26]

Early training was imperative. The different race of mothers that Scudder envisioned must begin to teach the coming generation to turn away from earthly chains in the cradle. He believed and preached that because Christian mothers were powerful instrumentalities for the conversion of the entire world they must infuse the missionary spirit in the heart of the rising generation at the earliest opportunity.

Referring to the Lockean *tabula rasa*, the idea that a child learns more by the time it is four years old than during all the rest of its life, Scudder informed mothers that their children's hearts "are like melted wax, and readily run into the moulds you make for them." Depending on his mother, a child can have a "martial or a peaceful character, a money-grasping or a generous one, a suspicious or a frank one." And he could enter the ministry or reject it. It was up to mother, and she ignored her charge to her everlasting peril. "Mothers who profess to be Christians but who are unwilling to have their sons enter the ministry…may expect to weep over ungodly sons, and break their hearts over graves on whose tombstones there shall be no record of hope," he warned.[27]

25. Abbott, ibid., pp. 125-138.
26. John Scudder, *An Appeal to Christian Mothers, in Behalf of the Heathen* (New York, 1844), pp. 6-8.
27. Scudder, *Appeal*, pp. 14, 63.

When did a mother's influence commence? The Rev. Thomas DeWitt, addressing the Female Sabbath School of the Collegiate Dutch Church in New York at its nineteenth anniversary celebration in 1835, told mothers that they should teach their children "as soon as they can lisp, their dependence on divine grace." But in an item titled, "When Does a Mother's Influence Commence?" the *Intelligencer* was of the opinion that her sway began even before the child's birth: "No one can tell how powerful are the impulses which her spirit communicates to it [in the womb]. She may be...forming a Jeremiah or John the Baptist."[28]

By her impressing upon her son's mind in infancy that he was meant for the Lord's work, "he will grow up with but one thought and one design...to live and labor for a dying world." Mothers were to furnish their sons with simple nursery books and periodical papers that drew their attention to the heathen and choose books for them that "in simple historical portraitures, display[ed] the grand reasons of the world's wretchedness." Eschew such frivolous and dangerous books as "Jack the Giant Killer," Scudder advised. Give children facts, not airy fancies.[29] Scudder's own *Letters to Sabbath-school Children on the Condition of the Heathen, Voice from the East,* and *Grand Papa's Talk with His Little Mary* perfectly fit these descriptions of preferred reading and were all best sellers.

Mothers had additional challenges. They were to teach their children when very young to contribute for the support of the gospel at home and among the heathen. Teach them to earn or save a penny and to give it to the Lord's treasury, Scudder exhorted. Finally, it was important that a mother let her son know she had consecrated him to God. "Take him alone...kneel with him; put your hand upon his head...and pray with him. Give him away to God, audibly...tell him you do not consider him your son, but God's; and frequently [remind] him of this...." A mother's duty was to kindle in her son's heart the heroic spirit of the gospel, to make the missionary enterprise appear so glorious that he would hunger to experience it himself. "Set before

28. *CI*, May 2, 1835; and August 11, 1870, p. 128.
29. Scudder, ibid., pp. 52-54. The idea that spiritual growth should start in the nursery is basic to Reformed doctrine and theology. It found popular expression in the writings of the Congregational minister Horace Bushnell, whose classic work, *Christian Nurture,* was first published in 1847. However, Reformed clergymen had been espousing the opinion that childhood was not merely a preparation for adulthood but an integral part of life long before Bushnell made it popular. See Fabend, "Suffer the Little Children," p. 27.

him the Captain of Salvation...that his heart may pant...to be one [of] Christ's soldiers."30

"O Christian mothers," Scudder concluded, "Bestir yourselves....The church looks to you with deep solicitude. The church of the coming generation has its germs in your families. You are the guardians over Christ's nursery. Shall they be plants standing like green olive-trees in the house of God, or shall they be like the present dwarfish race of christians [?]"31

John Scudder and his wife had eight sons, born between 1822 and 1848. Seven of them became ordained ministers in the Reformed Dutch Church, and the eighth died while in preparation. The Scudders were the evangelical parents par excellence.

"A moment & we are in eternity"

Many mothers in the Reformed faith readily accepted and struggled with the burdens placed on them for their family's spiritual condition. In 1870, at the tenth anniversary of the Mothers' Concert of Prayer in Brooklyn Heights (Dr. Zechariah Eddy's Church), "three great questions" were discussed: How can the conversion of our children be secured while they are in childhood? How can they be shielded from the evil that surrounds them? and How can they become so strong in Christianity as to be fitted for a life of self-sacrifice? In her address, Mrs. Rufus W. Clark of Albany, wife of the minister of the North Dutch Church there, spoke of God as having given to women "the highest gift, that of influence: it is a royal prerogative, more precious than a diadem...." Another speaker "dwelt upon self-government on the part of the mother as the essential requisite in the training of children and of consecration of [her own] heart as the only preparation for any Christian work." Mrs. Pruyn of Albany revealed to her colleagues that the death of her own son had moved her to become a mother to those that had none, and "now to consecrate the remainder of her life to the destitute children of Japan," which she did.32

But the burden of responsibility for their children's welfare not only in this life but in the life hereafter sorely taxed pious mothers as well, especially when their children showed signs of disobedience or of disaffection from the church. Some pious mothers had to face the very painful reality that their

30. Scudder, ibid., pp. 57-59.
31. Scudder, ibid., p. 64
32. *CI*, November 3, 1870, p. 176.

children were not susceptible to their redemptive powers and thus were not to inherit the Kingdom. "My beloved but wayward son," Mary Ann Gansevoort wrote to Stanwyx, age twenty-two, "Before your eyes ever saw the light of the sun, the most fervent prayers were put up at the Throne of Grace for you. [Your drunken behavior] grieves me when I think of the many ten thousand mercies I have done you...." She begs him to leave his evil friends and ask God's forgiveness.[33]

A series of nine deaths in five months in the family of Margaret Schenck Nevius in the Raritan area gave rise to terrible fears in her for the spiritual condition of her son, away at school: "While you are trying to store your mind with useful knowledge," she wrote to him, "may you get that Wisdom which cometh from above[.] choose Jesus as your friend then you will be happy put it not off for 'Now is the accepted time'...you know not that another day is yours....Oh my dear son how would I feel if I should get...word of you[r death]. Give your heart to the Saviour now...," she beseeched him.[34]

Phebe Davis, a member of the First Reformed Church in Somerville, New Jersey, shared with her cousin Margaret the feeling that "it is a consolation to parents to see their children follow...Christ....[I]f we could persuade the young to think, and examine their thoughts," she wrote, "they would soon be convinced their affections were not set on God[,] their kind and bountyfull benefactor, and as they must give an account to him of their thoughts and ways, they would know they must have one [intermediator] to stand between them and an offended God."[35]

Such letters, as well as diaries and spiritual narratives, funeral discourses and obituaries, articles, sermons, and journals that survive from this period make clear that many women suffered recurrent bouts of disquietude and doubt, severe nervous apprehension, depression, and psychosomatic illnesses that seem often to have been related to their anxieties regarding their children's spiritual condition. And many women—not only mothers, but aunts and grandmothers, ministers' wives and farmers' wives, maiden ladies and girls at school—suffered from feelings of their own spiritual deficiencies. Joanna Bethune, mother of the Reformed minister Dr. George Bethune, suffered concern for her "impenitent" grandchildren. Anna Lansing

33. Gansevoort-Lansing Collection, New York Public Library, Box 177, Folder 10, March 12, 1844.
34. Schenck Family Papers, RUL, May 30, 1864.
35. Cornelius C. Vermeule Papers, RUL, Box 4, correspondence folder.

Monteath, wife of a Reformed minister, wrote to her sister in 1828: "Tell [my nieces] from me the thread of life is brittle. A moment & we are in eternity....Oh I find as I travel along in this world that I have much to learn & very little time to learn it in—I wish very much to be a consistent useful humble Domine's wife, but oh how much is wanted for this...."[36]

Though she had no children, a Bergen County spinster, Maria Ferdon, agonized over the spiritual deficiencies of her brother and his wife and children, whose carefree, fun-loving ways she characterized as wicked and even Satanic. Not every pious woman whose letters and diaries survive recorded her moments of religious unbelief, but Maria Ferdon, for one, was consumed with hers. Am I saved? she asked over and again, sure that a "secret besetting sin somewhere," the "winter in her soul," and her "hard & unbelieving heart" disqualified her from ever attaining salvation. Though she recorded in 1876 that she had "twice seen the Lord in four weeks," the same day her unbelief caused her to abstain from Communion. Maria's particular conflict arose out of her inability to give up her belief in the doctrine of predestination. Though others could believe that "all go to heaven there is no hell," she could not.[37]

Spiritual anxiety did not decline in old age. The elderly Catherine Hardenberg received a letter from a friend in New Brunswick: "Now for [the] spiritual—tell me dear C——how is your heart revived?...tell me all about it for I am anxious to know why my heart cannot be warmed, I dont doubt my having grace any more than I would doubt yours, but you have more faith by your fruits...." Another aged friend wrote to Catherine: "I continually find a mar in my spirit, and...the good I would do—I do not, and so my wicked heart is continually in a ferment."[38]

Maria Frelinghuysen, wife of the Reformed Dominie John Cornell, and highly admired for her piety, was inclined throughout her life, according to her brother's biographer, "to seasons of religious darkness, when a deep sense of unworthiness clouded every prospect."[39] Indeed, Maria's own letters tell the story. At age fifty she wrote to her daughter: "Sometimes,

36. Mrs. Joanna Bethune, *Memoirs* (New York, 1863), p. 243; and Gansevoort-Lansing Collection, New York Public Library, Box 285, Folder 11, Feb. 28, 1828.
37. Maria Ferdon's unpublished diaries, Bergen County Historical Society.
38. Hardenbergh Family Papers, RUL, Folder 4, April 17, 1831, and Folder 4, Feb. 27, 1832.
39. Talbot W. Chambers, *Memoir of the Life and Character of the Late Honorable Theodore Frelinghuysen, LLD* (New York, 1862), p. 280.

Dear Anna, I can exercise a comfortable hope in that God, from whom I have received so many, so great, and so undeserved favors. Then again darkness and depondence [sic] seize my soul, and hold it in agonizing dread." And to her daughter Catharine she wrote, "I slept little last night, owing in some measure to a disturbed mind. We are frail creatures, My Dear Child, although God has given us exceeding great and precious promises, yet our unbelieving hearts prevent the application of them at all times." Two years before her death at age fifty-four she wrote to her son Frederick: "[May you never] have cause for those self-reproaches which so often torture the peace of your mother. When I review my past-life, oh what bitter reflections! How much neglected duty! How much committed evil! What abused privileges! What forgotten or disregarded Providences!...It seems to me I must still be classed among those who are in the gall of bitterness & the bonds of iniquity."[40] And this from one of the saintliest women in the denomination.

Reformed clergymen acknowledged the stresses on women and were quick to sympathize with their burdens. "The education of children," wrote the Rev. George Bethune in 1846, "is the most important, delightful, yet anxious duty of Christian parents. To train them up in useful religious knowledge for an honorable life here, and eternal life hereafter, requires the most watchful, patient, skilful care....No pious parent can contemplate the progress of a child toward maturity without deep solicitude....[Every] pious parent is harassed by conflicting extremes; and, after the utmost pains, [is] liable to severe disappointments, for both time and eternity."[41]

Though some unfortunate mothers had to acknowledge the failure of their redemptive powers, many were rejoiced by their successes. It was a great day when a mother knew that her children were safe in the knowledge of Christ's redeeming love—and a great day for the community. The Rev. Thomas De Witt Talmage, one of the giants of the Reformed church in the nineteenth century, reported how his grandmother in Somerville, New Jersey, prayed that her children might be saved, and they were saved, and the "news spread...and there was a great turning unto God; and over two hundred souls, in one day, stood up in the village church to profess faith in Christ."[42]

40. *Memoir of Maria Frelinghuysen Cornell, 1828.* Typescript, Gardner A. Sage Library, New Brunswick Theological Seminary.
41. George W. Bethune, *Early Lost, Early Saved. An Argument for the Salvation of Infants* (Philadelphia, 1846), p. 108.
42. Thomas De Witt Talmage, *Around the Tea-table* (Philadelphia, 1875), p. 440-441.

Loud rang the praises for those mothers who succeeded in bringing their children to the Lord. Jacob Chamberlain, a student at New Brunswick Theological Seminary, wrote to his mother in 1857 that he had just returned from the river banks where "concealed by clumps of cedar shrubs" he had spent the twilight hour on his knees commending his dear ones to God. "I am thankfull My dear Mother that you trained us from infancy to consider that hour sacred to that purpose, for however widely scattered we are we know that while we have a mother living her prayers are then ascending for us." And another student, of the Rutgers class of '66, wrote, "Nothing will sooner move the sensibilities of the hardest heart than the memory of a sainted mother." Mother is the child's first instructor, he wrote, and the domestic fireside a seminary of infinite importance, "the great institution of Providence for the education of man." How vast is a mother's power, "how limitless her dominion!…." And many were the testimonies at the world-famous Fulton Street Prayer Meeting in the Reformed church there to praying mothers. "I believe God was answering the prayer of that praying mother," testified one converted sinner, "when he led me by his Holy Spirit to think on the subject of religion."[43]

In the end, the pious mother's real power issued not from her ability to assert her authority over her children, or to inflict pain and guilt on them, but in the loving and selfless "ten thousand mercies" she showered upon them. Theodore Frelinghuysen credited the loving ways of his grandmother, Dina van den Bergh Hardenbergh, for leading him to the Saviour. "Though deservedly eminent for her piety, she was far from being austere, but, on the contrary, gracious and winning."[44] And "Be kind to thy mother," cautioned *Our Sabbath School Messenger* in one of hundreds of similar verses of the era, "for lo! on her brow,/May traces of sorrow be seen!/Oh, well may'st thou cherish and comfort her now,/ For loving and kind she has been."

The power of the evangelical Reformed Dutch mother reverberated for generations. Scudder had said in 1844, "In the cradles you rock lie infolded

43. Chamberlain Family Papers, New Jersey Historical Society, MG 1228, March 22, 1857. Jacob became a Reformed missionary. The Rutgers student wrote "Mother's Influence," an article in *Our Sabbath School Messenger*, a monthly publication of the Second Reformed Dutch Church in Philadelphia. Griffis Collection, RUL, p. 98. Though the article is signed only with the initials JGVS, in his copy of it, the editor, William E. Griffis, identified the author as J. G. Van Slyke. And *CI*, October 18, 1860, p. 66.
44. Chambers, *Memoir of Frelinghuysen*, p. 129.

the hopes of Christless nations." And thirty years later Talmage sounded the same theme: "The mother thinks she is only rocking a child, but...she may be rocking the fate of nations."[45] In fact, she did rock the fate of nations, especially her own nation: Her sons entered the ministry and the missionary field, her daughters married men determined to save the world from sin and took up the cause themselves, she and her children and grandchildren after her powered maternal and benevolent associations, female moral-reform movements, Sabbath schools, YMCA's, widows' and orphans' relief associations, Dorcas societies, Mite societies, and the abolition and temperance movements. And to the extent that pious Reformed Dutch women worked to change the world for the better through such organizations, they participated in what may be regarded as the most important series of events in the nineteenth century, for abolition and thus the Civil War may not have occurred had not conscientious evangelicals acted on their moral scruples.[46]

The children of the pious Reformed woman sang her praises. Accounts of her virtue, piety, and devotion to the salvation of her children are so numerous as to be uncountable. And her influence extended from the grave. Years after her funeral, Talmage remembered his grief for his own mother in an essay called, "Paradisaic Woman." "Dear mother! Beautiful mother! It was a cloudless day when, with heavy hearts, we carried her out to the last resting-place. The withered leaves crumbled under hoof and wheel...and the sun shone on the Raritan River until it looked like fire; but more calm

---

45. Scudder, *Appeal*, pp. 9-10; and Talmage, "Motherhood," in *Around the Tea-Table*, p. 129.
46. Evangelical religion "made Americans the most religious people in the world, molded them into a unified, pietistic-perfectionist nation, and spurred them on to those heights of social reform, missionary endeavor, and imperialistic expansionism which constitute the moving forces" of American history. McLoughlin, *The American Evangelicals*, p. 1. See also George M. Marsden, *The Evangelical Mind and the New School Presbyterian Experience* (New Haven and London, 1970); Timothy L. Smith, *Revivalism and Social Reform in Mid-Nineteenth-Century America* (Nashville, 1957); Charles I. Foster, *An Errand of Mercy: The Evangelical United Front, 1790-1837* (Chapel Hill, 1960); Ernest Lee Tuveson, *Redeemer Nation: The Idea of America's Millennial Role* (Chicago, 1968); Martin E. Marty, *Righteous Empire: The Protestant Experience in America* (New York, 1970); Robert Handy, *Christian America: Protestant Hopes and Historical Realities* (New York, 1971); and Paul Boyer, *Urban Masses and Moral Order in America, 1820-1920* (Cambridge, Mass., 1978).

and beautiful and radiant was the setting sun of that aged pilgrim's life."47

It was in her role as a pilgrim leading her children through the thorns and brambles of this life to their heavenly homeland that the power of the pious mother lay. Her children rose up and called her blessed, as the Proverbs had said they would, because of her unceasing efforts to save them from the torments of Hell.48

47. T. De Witt Talmage, "Paradisaic Woman," *The Marriage Ring: A Series of Discourses in Brooklyn Tabernacle* (New York, 1886), pp. 155-56.
48. With the rise of women's studies in the 1970s, scholarly attention began to be paid to the religious beliefs and behavior of women, and although none of this literature deals directly with women in the Reformed Church, or even with women in downstate New York or in New Jersey in the nineteenth century, Reformed women can be approached within the same historiographical context. Some of the now classic works of the 1970s and 1980s are, in chronological order, Carroll Smith-Rosenberg, "Beauty, the Beast, and the Militant Woman: A Case Study in Sex Roles and Social Stress in Jacksonian America," *American Quarterly* 23 (1971): 562-584; Nancy F. Cott, *The Bonds of Womanhood: "Women's Sphere" in New England, 1780-1835* (New Haven, 1977); Mary P. Ryan, "A Women's Awakening: Evangelical Religion and the Families of Utica, New York, 1800-1840," *American Quarterly* 30 (1978), 602-623; Paul E. Johnson, *A Shopkeeper's Millennium: Society and Revivals in Rochester, New York, 1815-1837* (New York, 1978); Mary P. Ryan, *Cradle of the Middle Class: The Family in Oneida County, New York, 1790-1865* (Cambridge, 1981); Barbara Leslie Epstein, *The Politics of Domesticity: Women, Evangelism, and Temperance in Nineteenth Century America* (Middletown, 1981); and Charles E. Hambrick-Stowe, *The Practice of Piety: Puritan Devotional Disciplines in Seventeenth-Century New England* (Chapel Hill, 1982). See also Gerald F. Moran and Maris A. Vinovskis, "The Puritan Family and Religion: A Critical Reappraisal," *William and Mary Quarterly* 39 (January 1982): 29-63.
    A study of the experience of Reformed women in New York and New Jersey in the nineteenth century should reveal how they dealt with and were affected by the ethnic image and cultural distinctiveness of the Reformed church.

VI
Is a "Joyful Death" an Oxymoron?: The Christina de Moen Van Raalte Story

Karsten T. Rumohr-Voskuil

Elton J. Bruins

[Christina Johanna de Moen Van Raalte] remained a silent, powerful support for the establishment of the settlement, which was dear to her heart, and of which she said gratefully, while sick in bed: God has saved me and all mine whom I have brought here during nearly twenty-five years, and He showed me more of His help than I could expect.

Albertus Van Raalte, writing of his deceased wife.[1]

In many instances a person's death can overshadow that person's life in historical memory. About the life of Christina de Moen Van Raalte, the early records of Holland, Michigan say little except to mention her as Albertus

1. Biographical sketch of Christina Van Raalte dated June 30, 1871, presumed by Albertus Van Raalte, Van Raalte Collection, box 1, folder 2, Calvin College Archives. Translation by Harry Boonstra.

Van Raalte's sick wife and mother of their eleven children. Death must indeed have been a relief from the physical pain of Christina Van Raalte's years of poor health. And for the Van Raalte clan themselves, in their strong Calvinistic faith that death was for her a rebirth, her funeral seems to have represented more of a starting point for future life than a time for retrospection. But the life of this Dutch-American pioneer has left some traces. In this essay, we will draw on family correspondence and other mid-nineteenth-century sources to point to two factors in the life of Christina Van Raalte that affected her greatly and can help show us who she was: her family interaction and her physical and emotional health. Although there is much that the sources do not tell us, still the evidence concerning those two factors is strong enough to suggest the framework of a portrait.

Life Before Death

Christina de Moen was born to an upper middle-class Protestant family in the Dutch city of Leiden January 30, 1815. She had two sisters and two brothers. Her father, Benjamin de Moen, died young, and it was her mother, Maria Wihelmina Menzel de Moen, who raised the children. The family were Separatist—that is, they supported the 1834 *Afscheiding*, or separation from the official state-sponsored church of the Netherlands—in spite of the hostile environment in which this placed them and in spite of their high socio-economic position.[2] The elder de Moen son, Carel Godefroi, became pastor of the Separatist Church at Den Ham, and all three daughters married leading Separatists: the eldest, Maria Wilhelmina, married Anthony Brummelkamp; the youngest, Johanna Christina, married S. Van Velzen; and Christina Johanna herself, the middle daughter, married Albertus Van Raalte.[3] According to family tradition, it was at some point during Albertus Van Raalte's theological study at Leiden (1834-35) that, after a local Separatist church service that was attended also by the de Moens, he called on the family at home and inquired specifically after Christina. Her relationship with Albertus evolved from this less-than-subtle inquiry. Their

---

2. Katherine Bratt, "Mrs. A. C. Van Raalte," the *Young Calvinist* 28 (11 November 1947): 26-27.
3. Albert Hyma, *Albertus C. Van Raalte and his Dutch Settlements in the United States* (Grand Rapids: Eerdmans, 1947), pp. 120-23 on Carel Godefroi, 31-33 on sisters' marriages. For the names of the sisters we are indebted to Elisabeth Dekker of the A.C. Van Raalte Institute of Historical Studies.

civil marriage was recorded in Leiden on March 11, 1836, and they received the official church blessing in Amsterdam on March 15.[4]

Between 1836 and the formation of the Holland Kolonie in Michigan in 1847, Albertus Van Raalte held pastorates in the Separatist churches of the Dutch towns of "Genemuiden, Mastenbroek, Ommen, and Arnhem on the Rhine."[5] These ten years of Separatist ministry proved costly to the Van Raaltes as the state government enforced its anti-Separatist decrees on the splinter movement: the young pastor was frequently jailed and the family endured various official harassment such as the billeting of soldiers in their parsonage.[6] It was during this time that, because of the religious persecution and other economic hardships, many Separatists began to emigrate to the United States; and Albertus Van Raalte became convinced of the need for direction and organization for the migration, and of his own calling to fill that need.[7] A twentieth-century writer has speculated on Christina's reaction: "Mrs. Van Raalte faced a great crisis in her life when her husband felt himself called of God to lead a group of his people as emigrants to America. How much it must have meant to Mrs. Van Raalte to bid farewell to her friends and relatives and her fatherland."[8]

On October 2, 1846, the Van Raalte family sailed for America, and in the following year they settled in Michigan. There, as parents of seven living children, Christina and Albertus combined leadership at home with civic and religious guidance of the Kolonie as the "first family" of Holland.[9] Their position of leadership, along with the wealth they derived from Albertus's business venture in the Netherlands, set this family apart from the majority of the working class in the Kolonie.[10] With large holdings of land and a

4. Jaap Pelgrim to Helena Visscher Winter, March 18, 1994, Van Raalte Institute. For a facsimile of the civil marriage certificate see Hyma, p. 34.
5. Bratt, p. 27; Hyma, pp. 33-40.
6. Bratt, p. 27.
7. On the migration of Separatists to the United States see, for instance: Henry S. Lucas, *Netherlanders in America* (reprint, Grand Rapids: Eerdmans, 1989), pp. 42-86; Jacob Van Hinte, *Netherlanders in America*. ed. Robert P. Swierenga, trans. Adriaan de Wit *et al.* (Grand Rapids: Baker, 1985), pp. 77-191.
8. Bratt, p. 27.
9. Six children were born to the Van Raaltes in the Netherlands and five in the United States. Of these, four—one in the Netherlands and three in the United States—died in childhood. Marie Zingle, "Children of Albertus Van Raalte and Christina de Moen" (1999), copy in Van Raalte Institute.
10. This business venture was a brick and tile factory originally owned by the de Moen family. Eventually, Carel de Moen turned the factory over to Albertus Van Raalte and the latter's sister's husband, Dirk Blikman Kikkert. When emigrating

"mansion" built for the family home on the east side of Holland, the Van
Raalte clan lived in a semi-isolation from the Kolonie.[11] This separation
from the town only strengthened family ties.

Family Interaction

Christina Van Raalte was in every sense of the word a family-oriented
person. Despite health problems, governmental harassment in the
Netherlands, less-than-ideal living conditions in the early days in the
Kolonie, and the radical change of lifestyle that the Kolonie required of her,
she remained involved with the lives of her children and husband.

The emotional attachment of Albertus for Christina Van Raalte is evident
in his loving correspondence with her. While serving churches in the
Netherlands he addressed her in terms such as, "dearly beloved wife," and
signed himself, for instance, "your loving and praying husband" —phrases
that suggest a private side of the Van Raalte relationship often unrecognized.[12]

But whereas for Albertus Van Raalte the family was one of many arenas
in which he placed his personal commitment, for Christina Van Raalte it was
the sole arena. The formation of the Kolonie brought Albertus into a leading
position as the religious and civic leader, intellectual pacesetter, and
financial backbone to the fledgling Dutch community. These responsibilities
for maintaining the "new Jerusalem" forced the minister to be away from the
family frequently—a fact that often brought a necessary uneasiness to the

to the United States, Albertus Van Raalte sold his share of the factory for 25,000
guilders. Elton J. Bruins, "Albertus Christiaan Van Raalte: Funding His Vision of
a Christian Colony," *The Dutch and their Faith*, Eighth Biennial Conference of
the Association for the Advancement of Dutch American Studies (Grand Rapids,
1991), pp. 53-63; Hyma, p. 123.

11. The Van Raalte family's first home in the Kolonie was a simple log house. The
"mansion" was their second home, the product of a series of additions that made
it one of the largest homes in the Kolonie, with twenty-one rooms, including eight
bedrooms and three living rooms, built with cherry wood and located on seven
and a half acres on the then extreme east side of Holland. Eventually, Hope
College demolished the mansion to make room for the Buys Athletic Fields. "The
Albertus C. Van Raalte Homestead," *Hope College Alumni Magazine* 1, no. 4
(January, 1948).

12. Albertus Van Raalte to Christina Van Raalte, May 1, 1837, Van Raalte Collection,
box 8, folder 107, Calvin College Archives. Translator unknown. In a letter of
October 2, 1837, Albertus wrote her, "Now my beloved wife, the Lord enlighten,
comfort and sanctify you...[signed] Your dearly loving husband." Van Raalte
Papers, box 8, folder 107, Calvin College Archives. Translator unknown.

family's interaction. For example, in a letter of December 1, 1859, he asked his friend Philip Phelps, then principal of the Holland Academy (the forerunner of Hope College), to help comfort his wife while he himself was in New York raising money. "Now I wish you to do your utmost to convince my wife about the necessity of my staving [sic] so long: I pray you convince her and if her mind is quiet I shall feel cheered very much."[13] Only nine days later, in the course of the same trip, Albertus remarked to Phelps that "a certain gentlemen did call the Holland Academy my first wife and Mrs. Van Raalte my second wife...."[14]

The attachment Mrs. Van Raalte had to her children is evident at the time when her sons Ben and Dirk wanted to enlist in the Union Army. In a letter of June 29, 1862, to Giles Van de Wal, a former instructor at the academy who was then a missionary in South Africa, Albertus explained why his two sons were not in the flannel blue uniforms. "My wife was almost frantic when the boys wanted to go and it was for her sake they didn't."[15] Eventually Ben and Dirk did enlist and were sent south to fight, but their mother's attachment to them lost no strength beyond the Mason Dixon Line. She would send her boys extra clothing in the mail even as they pleaded against this show of affection. Ben wrote, "If I need anything I will write for it. Mother must not send me anything unless I ask for it."[16]

Such letters present a picture of a mother and wife who was highly protective, easily worried, very loyal, and immensely caring. Her family was her true focal point. For her, family allegiance had priority over that attachment to friends and family in the Netherlands that made her departure difficult; family cohesiveness had priority over the ideology and nationalism that would have drawn her sons away; and, most symbolically, her allegiance to her husband's dream for the Utopia-like Kolonie of Holland had priority over her own health.

13. Albertus Van Raalte to Philip Phelps, December 1, 1859, Van Raalte Papers, Hope College Collection, Joint Archives of Holland.
14. Albertus Van Raalte to Philip Phelps, December 10, 1859, Van Raalte Papers, Hope College Collection, Joint Archives of Holland.
15. Albertus Van Raalte to Giles Van de Wal, June 29, 1862, Van Raalte Papers, Holland Historical Trust Collection, Joint Archives of Holland. Translation by Clarence Jalving.
16. Benjamin Van Raalte to Albertus Van Raalte, July 14, 1864, from the camp of the 25th Michigan, located near the Chattahoochee River in Georgia. Van Raalte Papers, Holland Historical Trust Collection, Joint Archives of Holland. Translation by Clarence Jalving.

Deteriorating Health

To understand Christina Van Raalte one must study not only her family interaction but also the emotional and physical trauma that accompanied it. For there is no doubt that she lived her adult life with considerable health problems.

The historical evidence of such problems can be found as early as May 12, 1837, when Albertus Van Raalte wrote to his wife of one year, wishing that "the Lord also grant you, if possible, your health again." Though the letter lacks any description of her illness, it presages the deterioration of her health.[17]

In later letters Albertus often spoke of her as ill. Four years after the founding of the Kolonie in western Michigan she seems to have come close to death at the relatively early age of thirty-six; on December 10, 1851, Albertus wrote to John Garretson of the Board of Domestic Missions, "My wife has been very sick and in great danger but the Lord did have pity on me and did give her back."[18] By May 17, 1853, in another letter to Garretson, he was using the phrase "very sick and feeble" to describe his suffering wife.[19] In 1860, he wrote to his good friend and confidant Phelps, referring to her as "always exhausted and overworking and often unwell,"[20] and two months later remarked that she "is up and doing but complaining and very feeble."[21]

In 1866, when the couple took their first trip back to the Netherlands to see friends and family, they also hoped for an improvement of Mrs. Van Raalte's health. There were signs of improvement; in a letter from the city of Kampen, Albertus wrote Phelps, "Mrs. Van Raalte was much exhausted, also by the sensation of meeting their friends and relations, but I see [a]

17. Albertus Van Raalte to Christina Van Raalte, May 12, 1837, Van Raalte Papers, box 8, folder 107, Calvin College Archives. Translator unknown.
18. Albertus Van Raalte to John Garretson, December 10, 1851, Correspondence of the Board of Domestic Missions, box 10, folder for September-December 1851, Archives of the Reformed Church in America, New Brunswick, New Jersey.
19. Albertus Van Raalte to John Garretson, May 17, 1853, Correspondence of the Board of Domestic Missions, box 11, folder for April-June, 1853, Archives of the Reformed Church in America.
20. Albertus Van Raalte to Philip Phelps, August 31, 1860, Van Raalte Papers, Hope College Collection, Joint Archives of Holland.
21. Albertus Van Raalte to Philip Phelps, September 24, 1860, Van Raalte Papers, Hope College Collection, Joint Archives of Holland.
22. Albertus Van Raalte to Philip Phelps, May 24, 1866, Van Raalte Papers, Hope College Collection, Joint Archives of Holland. Translation by Clarence Jalving.

recovering of her strength…."[22] A month later, in a letter to his son Ben, he used even more optimistic language: "Mother and I are both well—Mother's stomach has been a little upset but it is nothing serious. It seems to me that Mother has already gained weight and her cough is better so we have much to be thankful for."[23] This trip to the Netherlands appears to have been the only true break from the deteriorating physical and emotional factors causing Christina Van Raalte's slide towards death.

In early 1869, Albertus Van Raalte again tried to colonize a new Dutch settlement, this time in Amelia, Virginia. Even though this move to a less erratic climate was supposed to be beneficial to Christina, it was not in her best interest. Albertus wrote to his son, "Mother is going to write this week also. She is reasonably good health although I sometimes fear for her. She misses the family, is bothered with rheumatism and frequently has cramps at night."[24] In later 1869, the family moved back to the Kolonie in Michigan. The seriousness of the deterioration in Christina's health is evident in an emotional letter that Albertus addressed to Phelps in 1870. "I have not been mingling in Town nor in any business since I last saw you," he wrote. "But yet my hands are full, especially with watching my wife: my anxieties are on the increase and yet I am hoping. However it looks gloomy: the summer is nearly past and we have lost much. I dread the winter!"[25]

Only months before her death, Mr. Van Raalte again wrote to Mr. Phelps, saying, "Mrs. Van Raalte is suffering: the fevers are destroying the vitality. Some times I see spells of easyness [sic] which makes me hope against common sense."[26] She died June 30, 1871.[27]

Life After Death

There is much we do not know about Christina Johanna de Moen Van Raalte. The complexities of her transition from a cultured, upper-middle-

23. Albertus Van Raalte to Benjamin Van Raalte, June 11, 1866, Van Raalte Papers, Holland Historical Trust Collection, Joint Archives of Holland. Translation by Clarence Jalving.
24. Albertus Van Raalte to Benjamin Van Raalte, May 4, 1869, Van Raalte Papers, Holland Historical Trust Collection, Joint Archives of Holland. Translation by Clarence Jalving.
25. Albertus Van Raalte to Philip Phelps, August 30, 1870, Van Raalte Papers, Hope College Collection, Joint Archives of Holland. Translation by Clarence Jalving.
26. Albertus Van Raalte to Philip Phelps., March 12, 1871, Van Raalte Papers, Hope College Collection, Joint Archives of Holland. Translation by Clarence Jalving.
27. Bratt, p. 27.

class lifestyle to a forest and swamp in the middle of nowhere, in which she fought physical illness while raising seven children with an eager husband are apparent enough. But the means by which she handled, or did not handle, these complexities are well hidden, and existing evidence is ambiguous. There are reports that she lived with a degree of depression, while other reports present her as a "saint" who easily interacted with others in the Kolonie, teaching the other pioneer women how to make bread on the open fire, or undertaking personally to clean the academy, or being chosen to decorate the Pillar Church after it was erected in 1856.[28]

A certain emphasis in the sources on what transcends this life, rather than on this life itself, may contribute to our lack of knowledge. Early in their marriage already, Albertus Van Raalte wrote to his wife of the value of release through physical death. "We will only be here for a short time," he told her, "before we will be leaving everything behind, and what if we would not have a treasure in heaven! Therefore we should value the one necessity higher than the instability, and insignificance, and the precariousness of the world. God our Lord will detach you from this work and give you insight in spiritual life through His divine light."[29]

But even in the absence of those many details of her life that we do not know, still we are far from ignorant about her. For the theme of her devotion to and interaction with family and the theme of her suffering and deteriorating health emerge clearly from the sources to suggest the factors that help determine her particular role within the story of the formation and cultivation of the Kolonie—a role that will merit more consideration, as we reflect in coming years on the historic importance of women in the Reformed Church in America.

28. Joanne Tharin, "Mrs. Christina Johanna de Moen Van Raalte," unpublished paper, Van Raalte Institute.
29. Albertus Van Raalte to Christina Van Raalte, May 1, 1837, Van Raalte Papers, box 8, folder 107, Calvin College Archives.

VII
The Rise of the Woman's Board of Foreign Missions

Russell L. Gasero

From the mid nineteenth century until recent decades, the work of church women in most American denominations was focused in local missionary societies — Ladies Aid Societies, Women's Guilds, Women's Auxiliaries, or similar groups — attached to denominational boards or societies. Even though they made significant contributions to the church, both financially and otherwise, these groups' work has been seen as auxilliary, rather than part of the mainstream of the church's life. Yet I think the case can be made that the development of the women's mission organizations marked an awakening of the church to the slow understanding that women have jobs to do, gifts to share, and calls to answer that are as varied and diverse as those of men had been up to that time. By way of making that case, the present essay will examine the early years of the Woman's Board of Foreign Missions of the Reformed Church in America.

Beginnings

As Mary E. A. Chamberlain pointed out in her semi-centennial history in 1925 of the Woman's Board of Foreign Missions (WBFM), the roots of the organization may be traced at least forty years before its founding in 1875, especially in the contributions of two earlier Reformed church figures who had pioneered in women's mission work. These were David Abeel and Sarah Doremus.[1] Abeel (1804-46), ordained by the Classis of New Brunswick as an evangelist in 1826, began his career as pioneer missionary to China and Southeast Asia in 1829. He saw that in Asia as in in most other mission areas at the time, women alone had access to their own sex, and so he began to call for the women of the church to organize for the aid of women in foreign lands. In England in 1834 he wrote an influential appeal for the first independent women's missionary society, the so-called "Society for Promoting Female Education in China and the East," and later that year made similar pleas for (as he put it) "women's work for women" in the United States, calling attention to the degraded condition of women in China, with particular focus on practices such as footbinding, and emphasizing the need for unmarried volunteers in the field.[2] Partly in response to his pleas, local societies of women — often called Cent or Mite Societies, because the cost of membership was one cent per week — emerged to support and encourage "women's work for women." Sarah Doremus (d. 1877) was a member of the South Dutch Church in New York City. She herself had bid Abeel farewell on his departure to Asia in 1829 and helped arrange his meetings with mission-minded women in New York five years later. She looked after the comfort of many departing and arriving missionaries throughout her lifetime. And in 1861, it was she who organized the first ecumenical women's missionary organization in America, which was called the Women's Union Missionary Society.[3]

When the "Woman's Board of Foreign Missions" was established in 1875, on the basis of a General Synod resolution of the previous year, it was very much in the spirit of Abeel and Doremus. The minutes of the first meeting, held January 7 at Marble Collegiate Church, suggest the zeal of those attending:

1. Mary E. A. Chamberlain, *Fifty Years in Foreign Fields. China, Japan, India, Arabia. A History of Five Decades of the Woman's Board of Foreign Mission, Reformed Church in America* (New York: Women's Board of Foreign Missions, 1925), pp. 3-8.
2. Alvin J. Poppen. "The Life and Work of David Abeel," unpublished S.T.M. thesis, Union Theological Seminary, 1959.
3. For Information on Sarah Doremus see Una Ratmeyer, *Hands, Hearts, and Voices: Women Who Followed God's Call* (New York, 1995), pp. 2-4, and James I. Good, *Women of the Reformed Church* (n.p., 1901), pp. 287-95.

The day was an extremely unpleasant one. Rain was falling rapidly, and froze as it touched the side walks so that it was very difficult to traverse the streets. Yet the ladies present had come from Hackensack, N.J., Brooklyn, L.I., Yonkers, Millbrook, Saugerties, N.Y. and Belleville, N.J.[4]

They went to work immediately, adopting articles of a temporary constitution and appointing a board of managers, who then attended a subsequent organizational meeting January 21, which adopted a permanent constitution. The purpose of the new organization, as set forth in that document, was to aid the synod's Board of Foreign Missions by promoting its work among the women and children of foreign mission fields, "to which end it strives to increase the interest in this work among the women of the churches at home, and through funds collected by auxiliary societies to support schools established by synod's board, as well as medical and evangelistic work for the women and children at the mission stations."[5] Disbursement of money they collected was subject to the approval of the synod's board.

The Work of the Woman's Board of Foreign Missions

From the start, the board's leaders gave high priority to publication. They knew the best way to promote the mission effort was through effective communication designed to elicit supportive response. Already in 1877 the board published its *Manual of Missions,* which included a history of all foreign mission work up to that date. It began as well to publish leaflets of letters from missionaries with illustrations. Such materials could be used at meetings of the auxiliaries to inform and inspire the work of the local groups. (Indeed, much use was made of missionary letters; many of the letters preserved in the RCA archives show the marks of editors who condensed them for publication of various types.) The WBFM also published its own periodical, the *Mission Gleaner* (as discussed by Renée House in this volume) and, from 1897, the *Day Star,* a children's paper that by 1905 had a circulation of 12,000 copies.

4. Archives of the Reformed Church in America (Archives, RCA), *Minutes of the Woman's Board of Foreign Missions,* vol. 1 p. 13.
5. Louise Chambers Knox, "History of the Woman's Board of Foreign Missions," *Christian Intelligencer* 76, no. 23 (June 7, 1905): 356-357.

Various special projects were also put into effect. The project known as the "Baby Roll," begun in 1897, was designed to encourage teaching children from infancy to give to the cause of Christ; the mother would promise, in her child's name, to contribute twenty-five cents a year for five years. Another was the "Summer Sewing Guild," started in 1895 to use the skills and talents of women to supply missionaries with needed clothing for distribution at their discretion through the mission schools, hospitals, and churches. Another project was the establishment in 1900 of a "Young Women's Branch," among whose members were some who themselves would answer the call to the mission field.[6]

Crucial to the work of the WBFM was the establishment of auxiliary societies in local congregations, as called for by the constitution. The board also enlisted help on the classical level, appealing in 1881 to each classis to appoint committees of two to supplement the correspondence of the corresponding secretary and to reach those congregations which failed to respond to appeals and correspondence. These committees' responsibility was to visit congregations within the classical boundaries and make personal appeals to individual members to form auxiliaries.[7] Missionary unions were also established in almost all classes. These unions "are the battlegrounds of the missionary at home on furlough, and the representative directly from the Board at home, conquering doubt, disseminating information and inspiring praiseworthy rivalry among the churches to "owning a missionary.""[8]

The WBFM thus worked in a variety of ways to give women a direct, visible role in the mission field of the church. In its scope and vision, this work was something new and really quite remarkable; for even though the idea of women's support for missions in the RCA antedated the WBFM, there had been nothing like this before in the denomination to mobilize individuals in such numbers, and in such a variety of ways, to participate genuinely in the global work of the church.

A Local Auxiliary

The RCA archives has many records of the local auxiliary groups of the WBFM. These records, though often sketchy, can give us some idea of the ways in which women on the local level were really affected by the spirit of

6. Ibid., p. 357.
7. Ibid., p. 357.
8. Ibid., p. 357.

the WBFM, and in turn affected their congregations. The records of one of the auxiliary of the Reformed Church in Readington, New Jersey, which was one of the first to be organized, provide a good example.

The minutes show from the beginning a highly organized effort. At the first meeting, held April 8, 1875. after opening prayer by the pastor of the congregation (J. H. Smock), the women elected Mrs. Smock, the pastor's wife, as president, and four other women — two married, two single — as the executive committee. The group decided to hold meetings on the first Thursday of each month. The annual dues were to be twenty-five cents and members were to contribute an additional ten cents (soon reduced to five cents) at each meeting, all to be forwarded to the national board. The group also appointed five different committees to visit the "various districts of the congregation, for the purpose of soliciting members."[9]

There is much that the records do not tell us. Particularly after the third monthly meeting, at which the group adopted the name "Faithful Sowers," the minutes begin to disappoint our desire for specifics. From then on, they record a similar routine from meeting to meeting, each of which opened with prayer and song and proceeded to discussion of communications to the board and the collection of dues. The minutes have a solemn tone, and brevity was apparently thought beautiful. There is no substantive comment on what was said, what goals were set before them, or what missions they took particular interest in and why.

But even though the minutes are silent about many things we would like to know, they do witness clearly to the organization's quick success in attracting members and funds. By the end of the first year, membership had increased from thirteen to 130 members. Solicitation within the geographical districts had resulted in a collection of $150. When the group began to take a special interest in the building of a school in Nagasaki, they were able to make a designated gift of between $100 and $200 annually.[10]

The records also suggest that in point of fact mission support was not the only purpose of the auxiliary; the group also, as we might well expect, helped meet the social needs of its members, perhaps particularly (as I shall suggest) those who were unmarried. It may be that no one thought about the social dimension of the group at the moment of organization, but this soon

9. Archives, RCA, Women's Missionary Society Minutes, vol. 1, Readington Reformed Church, Readington, N.J. (WMSM-R), April 8, 1875.
10. WMSM-R, summarizing the annual reports.

made itself felt. Already the [first?] annual report acknowledged that meetings dedicated purely to the collecting of money for the cause were not particularly popular, and that it might be well not to put so much emphasis on dues.

> Our meetings thus far have been called mainly for the purpose of collecting monthly dues, and consequently, no special interest has been manifested in them. In fact it was thought advisable to discontinue them altogether during the Winter. Nothwithstanding this, we feel that we have accomplished something which under the blessing of our Heavenly Father, whose kingdom we are laboring to extend, will be instrumental of great and constantly increasing good."[11]

In 1876 it was decided to constitute the meetings as "sociables," i.e., occasions for fellowship and education, rather than for the transaction of business alone. The meetings would begin at eight and close at eleven. All who were not members were to pay an admission fee of ten cents, to be forwarded to a mission designated by the national board. Such "sociable" meetings mainly consisted of entertainment, including lectures from visiting missionaries and others, readings, and singing, in mixtures that varied from meeting to meeting. The meetings ended with refreshments either in the home of a member or in the basement of the church. Sociables continued to be held at various members' houses with respectable attendance: The collections for these meetings was between $2.30 and $2.60, thus indicating a probable presence of from twenty-four to forty-eight women. It would appear that the majority of the women involved in the society were not married; of the list of names of officers and committee members at the April 6 annual meeting, three were married and ten were single. In August, 1876, the women expanded the idea of the sociable by holding a "festival" in a wooded area belonging to a member of the church. This seems to have been an all-day affair, much like a church picnic today, with committees established for tables, ice cream, lemonade, and candies, nuts, etc. The fact that these committees were entirely composed of men suggests that the auxiliary's sociability extended beyond its own membership.[12]

11. WMSM-R, Report for the year 1875.
12. WMSM-R, August 2, 1877.

The Readington auxiliary's records also show, early on, its potential importance for the support of the local congregation. Financial troubles hit Readington in the late 1870s, and at first, apparently, the women felt the need to defend their efforts to raise money for foreign missions when local needs were pressing. "We labor under considerable opposition, but our trust is in the Lord and we are working for the advancement of his Kingdom."[13] But in 1878 they decided, after much discussion, that "half the proceeds of Sociables held by the Society, between Oct. and Apr. of the present year be donated to the church, for the purpose of reducing the debt thereon."[14] (It is important to note here that the women were not voting members of the church.) Although in the next year, the local crisis having passed, they directed their collections once again to the missions of the board, they had demonstrated both their willingness to direct their support to the congregation itself and (perhaps more importantly) the congregation's need of them.

Laconic as they are, the Readington records thus show women not only engaged in foreign and domestic mission efforts, but also taking on important roles in the life of their congregation, both socially and financially. These and the many other similar local auxiliary records for the early period of the WBFM could be to be profitably studied with with an eye to the broader implications of the board's enterprise. Did the work of this board materially affect the role of women in the local church, and perhaps by implication in local society as well?

Conclusion: Missions Leading the Way

Throughout the records and literature of the WBFM, there is abundant evidence that the women involved were on the whole satisfied with their work and had positive feelings about its effect on the overall work of the kingdom. The tone of the Readington annual report in 1879 is typical.

> When we consider the great work in which we are engaged and the importance of sending the Gospel to our Sisters who 'sit in darkness,' we feel more than repaid for any self-denial we have been called to exercise.[15]

13. WMSM-R, Report for the year 1877.
14. WMSM-R, September 26, 1878.
15. WMSM-R, Report for the year 1879.

Such positive feeling may seem to us ironic, when we reflect that at the same time women were not allowed to serve either on consistories or in the ordained ministry — in other words, that they were excluded from the offices of the very church they served. But on the other hand the positive spirit of these women may be an indication of how missions have led the church. For missions, in this case foreign missions, have not only served as a unifying force amid the diversity that was and is the Reformed Church in America; they have also propelled the church forward, obliging it to reflect on its calling as the people of God. The women of the WBFM, after all, devoted their energies to the support of female missionaries, who in turn were demonstrating themselves to be the church's great pioneers in assuming positions of weighty, visible, and indeed "official" responsibility—precursors of the women who would receive ordination only several decades later. In that sense, when when we look at the women of the early WBFM, we are seeing the future.

VIII
Women Raising Women:
The Urgent Work of the
Mission Gleaner, 1883-1917

Renée S. House

A few years ago, the Commission on Women of the Reformed church began publishing a newsletter which they called *Gleanings*. They took this name from an earlier RCA women's publication called the *Mission Gleaner* about which the members of the commission actually knew very little, apart from the title. This prompted someone from the commission to call and inquire, "What can you tell us about the *Mission Gleaner*"? At that point I couldn't tell her very much, but being a good librarian, I promised to do some research and get back to her soon. In fact, I had wondered about this small women's magazine myself, so I spent part of that very afternoon sitting on the basement floor of the Gardner A. Sage Library reading through the earliest issue of this publication, which was prepared and distributed by the RCA Woman's Board of Foreign Mission between 1883 and 1917.

In the very first issue published, I came across a piece entitled, "A Plea for Help from the Little Widows of India to the Children of America." The following excerpt from that widow's plea gives an immediate sense of the tone and nature of much of the material published in the *Mission Gleaner*:

I am as young as some of you who call yourselves children, and yet I am a widow. They call me a widow because the man I was to have married, but whom I never saw, was taken sick and died. You cannot think what a dreadful thing it is to be a widow in India....From the day that her husband dies, the life of the widow is one of misery and oppression.... I overheard the missionary tell of a God who pities the widow, who loves the orphan and who forgives the sinner; who invites all who mourn and are in sorrow to come to Him...Is it true that He will even pity poor me—I who have no money, no jewels to pay Him for His kindness? I am only eight years old.... Now that I am a widow, I shall always live as one who is to be despised and scorned. That is the custom of my country. Oh, you who know of a God who will help me in my loneliness, send me word how I can find Him, for of all the gods we worship never one has said, "I am the God of the widow."[1]

I believe we can safely conclude that this plea was not written by an eight year-old-girl from India. It may have been written by the magazine's editor or another member of the Woman's Board, or borrowed from another source designed to inspire support for world missions. Although this plea tells part of the truth about the general situation of many young widows in India, the point of the little widow's story was not to report on an actual occurrence but rather to evoke a compassionate and immediate response to the urgent work of women missionaries on behalf of other women. The women who contributed to the *Gleaner* perceived that through their efforts on the homefront, they were a part of the church's missionary work to "heathen" women. They were partners with their sisters in the field, helping to raise up hundreds of thousands of poor and oppressed foreign women whose stories would be told on the pages of the *Gleaner*. In order to raise up these women, they would need to raise the interest and support of all their sisters in the RCA.

This magazine was to be the primary means of "keeping the women of the Church at home informed of the progress of the work on the field."[2] The Woman's Board believed that if the women of the church were ignorant of "what was actually being accomplished with the money" they contributed,

1. The *Mission Gleaner* 1, no. 1 (November/December 1883), pp. 7-8.
2. Mary E. A. Chamberlain, *Forty Years in the Foreign Field*, (New York: Woman's Board of Foreign Missions, Reformed Church in America), p. 34.

no "permanent interest" in foreign missions could be maintained.[3] The ultimate goal of the *Gleaner* was to prompt the women of the church to give more and more money for missions.

The magazine was written entirely for women, by women, and, mostly, about women. For the most part, the *Gleaner* is composed of excerpts from letters written by female missionaries to the women's board, to close friends in the States, and to women's auxiliaries and children's mission bands; endless stories about girls, boys, and women who are exemplars of the appropriate response to Christian missions; numerous detailed reports on the activities and meetings of women's auxiliaries and classical unions—the scriptures they read, the hymns they sang, the titles of the papers that were read and the names of the women and men who read them; and practical tips on how to organize and energize women, girls and boys for mission work.

Since I first opened the worm-eaten cover of the *Mission Gleaner* I have studied twelve years of the magazine, from 1883 to 1895, and have come to believe that it opens an important window into the lives and thoughts of Reformed church women during this late Victorian period. This essay is a report on work which is still very much in progress, but I hope it will convey some sense of what this woman's publication was intended to do and provide some perspective on the lives of Reformed church women and the church as a whole during this period.

The *Gleaner* is like an old attic full of trinkets and treasures, each of which has a story to tell. There is not space enough to tell them all here, but, taken together, these writings by, for, and about women begin to show something of the whole. In what follows, I will discuss three areas about which the *Gleaner* provides significant information and insight: (1) RCA women's interpretations of biblical texts which made sense of their own experience and helped justify their work for foreign missions; (2) the cultural assumptions which were offered in support of women's missionary work for women and the strategies the magazine used to motivate Reformed church women to respond to this work; (3) the successes and frustrations the women encountered in their attempts to organize and raise support on the homefront.

"Interpreting the Bible"

First then, the biblical texts which were offered by women, to women, to help them understand their experience and to justify their work for mission.

3. Ibid.

We can begin with the magazine's title—the *Mission Gleaner*. It points to a primary biblical story that made some sense of their experience and work on behalf of missions. Even before the *Gleaner* was published, the women identified themselves with Ruth, the gleaner. In 1878, the Board of Foreign Missions of the RCA (the men's board) began publishing the *Mission Monthly*. One-quarter of the space in that publication was given to the woman's board so that they could keep the church's women informed. The woman's board explained their purpose in the first issue of the *Mission Monthly* as follows: "...we are the *daughter of the Board of Foreign Missions of the Reformed Church in America*. As such it is our place and pleasure to stand by her in whatever she undertakes for the furtherance of the cause. We do not desire any money from those who have always contributed to her support, but we do hope, by our exertions in gleaning after her to relieve her of the care of some of her missionary family."[4]

When the *Gleaner* began as an autonomous publication of the woman's board in 1883, the women reiterated in their annual board report their intent to be "a gleaner, not a reaper in the field of the churches which belong by inheritance to Synod's Board."[5] But on the pages of the *Gleaner* itself, this publication by and for women only, there is never any further explanation of this title. It appears to me that the woman's board identified themselves with Ruth, at least in part, as a means of signaling to the men their intent to stay in their proper place in relation to the men's board. The women do not claim to own the field, or to have planted the seeds, or to be the primary laborers in the harvest. Like Ruth, the women signal their intent to remain in their rightful place.

But, Ruth was more than just a gleaner. Ruth also provided a perfect model of one who will remain faithful to the family. Like Ruth, these RCA women signal their intent to remain faithful to their church family — to the men's board, to the missionaries, and to those unknown and far away who by their conversion to Christ will become brothers and sisters in the faith. Like Ruth in maintaining their proper place, like her in swearing faithfulness, I suspect that some members of the woman's board also hoped to be like Ruth in another way. As she was recognized by Boaz, they hoped to be

4. *Mission Monthly* 1, no. 1 (April 1878), pp. 13-14.
5. Woman's Board of Foreign Missions of the Reformed Church in America. Tenth Annual Report, 1884, p. 11.

recognized by the church's male leaders for their diligence, faithful labor, and success in raising funds to increase the harvest of the church's mission.

On the pages of the *Gleaner*, the women told other biblical stories and invited the reader to see herself in them. One woman, in an enthusiastic response to the Ladies Day which was held during the 1889 meeting of the General Synod, writes, "God has honored woman. As on the resurrection morning Mary was given the message, 'go tell my brethren,' so have we a commission, the execution of which will bring the answer to the prayer of the morning, 'Bless us that through us many may be blessed.'"[6] She claims for church women both Mary's story and Abraham's story, who was blessed to be a blessing. Christ's Easter morning commissioning of women is cited again by a group of female missionaries justifying the work of women evangelists and calling for more women to do the work:

> It is not claimed that the evangelization of women cannot be done at all by the men — but there is more of it than men can do, there is much of it that will never be done unless women do it, and much that men cannot do as well as women can. There is nothing in this kind of work transcending the recognized scriptural sphere of women. Women received from the Lord Himself, upon the very morning of his resurrection, their commission to tell the blessed story of a risen Saviour. What they did then we may continue to do now.[7]

Christ's "Great Commission" is cited by Miss L. Arcularius in a paper concerning the church's educational work for women which was first presented at the annual missionary convention of the Westchester classes and subsequently published in the *Gleaner*. With conviction she says, Jesus Christ has "wonderfully prepared the way and opened the door of entrance to every nation of the earth" so that missionaries may "Go into all the world and preach the Gospel to every creature." She revels in the thought that "this Gospel, which we preach and which we believe, makes no distinctions; to women as well as men is the 'word of salvation sent'...the Lord graciously promises to bring not only sons from far, but daughters also from the ends of the earth. With such encouragements, and with unbounded faith in the

6. The *Mission Gleaner* 6, no. 5 (July/August 1889): p. 4.
7. The *Mission Gleaner* 7, no. 6 (September/October 1890): p. 4.

word of God, the Church of Christ goes forth in the footsteps of the Master...."[8]

Female missionaries offered other biblical stories for reflection. Writing from India, Mary Scudder describes the streets, houses, and community wells which remind her of how Jesus sat and asked for water from the Samaritan woman. Scudder asks, "Think you that it was an accident that He sat there waiting to give her the living water? Ah, no! His heart yearned for her soul, as it does for these our sisters now! Shall we let him watch alone?"[9] She invites the women to identify themselves with Jesus, whose heart also yearned for the salvation of a foreign woman.

A final illustration comes from a member of the woman's board, who in response to the 1889 General Synod's commendation of their accomplishments, was moved to reflect on the role of the church's women. For the readers of the *Gleaner* she recalls the words of the Creator, "It is not good for man to be alone" and goes on to interpret the story of Adam and Eve:

> "Each has a part and a totally different part of the same work. Woman can lay foundation work in the family, among the mothers which man cannot, may not do, and woman can give those touches, the 'broidery work' which makes the perfect, harmonious whole. So let the Woman's Board rejoice in being co-laborers with the grand body of ministers of the Reformed Church in America and come to their help next June with a report of twenty thousand dollars for the treasury!...I was going to shout, Hurrah!—but, being women, we will sing Hallelujah! [10]

It was perhaps a bit dangerous to identify the woman's board with Eve, but the attempt was to claim for women the place of colaborers with men. And although one gets the sense that the women were in a somewhat subordinate role as helpers of the men, they are standing alongside the men, rather than gleaning the fields behind them. I could offer many more examples of the women's use of the Bible to interpret their experience and that of the women who were served by the mission, but time will not allow it. Let me conclude this section by stressing the importance of these examples in

8. The *Mission Gleaner* 3, no. 1 (November/December 1885): 4-5.
9. The *Mission Gleaner* 3, no. 4 (May/June 1886): 10.
10. The *Mission Gleaner* 6, no. 5 (July/August 1889): 7-8.

helping us see that the *Gleaner* provided an outlet for women's interpretations of the Bible and provided for the possibility that these understandings of the biblical text would impact the lives of other women.

Interpreting the Culture

The second area I wish to focus on has to do with the cultural assumptions which were offered in support of women's missionary work for women and some of the strategies the magazine used to motivate Reformed church women to respond. the *Gleaner* shows that the church's women understood the importance of women's missionary work to other women in the terms handed to them by the Victorian culture of which they were a part. During this period, women were heralded as the most powerful sources for the spiritual and moral reform of society.[11] The center of their reforming work was in the home. Here it was expected that a woman's strong and gentle influence would raise children (especially girls) who would also exert high moral influence in the world. It was assumed that by their very nature, girls and women were more given to virtue than boys and men. Thus, girls and women would be responsible to be vigilant in keeping their brothers, sons and husbands from succumbing to the evil temptations which they found so hard to resist, and to provide virtuous examples for them to follow.

These attitudes about women and their power to influence toward the good are quite plainly stated in the *Gleaner* through the writings of female missionaries, students of the RCA's mission schools, and women from other mission societies. Writes Mrs. Smith of the Woman's American Baptist Missionary Society:

> The mothers and the homes are centers of power the world over....
> It follows then that a people cannot be civilized until the mothers
> are reached, and as mothers can only be reached by women, the
> Women's Boards are the greatest evangelizing force of the day.[12]

I am certain the the members of the RCA woman's board smiled over this one. Similar sentiments to those just quoted were most often expressed by

11. See Sara Evans, *Born for Liberty*, (New York, 1989); Barbara J. MacHaffie, *Her Story: Women in Christian Tradition*, (Philadelphia, 1986), pp. 93-106; Barbara Welter, "The Cult of True Womanhood, 1820-1860," in *Dimity Convictions: The American Woman in the Nineteenth Century* (Athens, Ohio, 1976), pp. 21-41.
12. The *Mission Gleaner* 7, no. 4 (1890): 5-6.

women in the Japan Mission. Miss Leila Winn was happy to report "a growing desire to have educated daughters, and there seems to be an awakening to the needs of female education. I love to see the women of Japan fully awakened to their responsibilities as wives and mothers."[13] One of the first graduates of Ferris Seminary in Japan responded to the question, "should women be educated?" with these words:

> Does not the fact that they are to be the future wives and mothers of men entitle them to the best culture Japan's young civilization can afford? Will not the homes over which they must preside be efficient in generating society and ridding the country of existing flagrant vices?[14]

The young student had learned these principles from the American female missionaries who taught her. Roughly ten years later, Lizzie B. Disbrow Harris, who served in the Japan Mission with her husband, Howard, shared her sense of marked progess in the "intelligence and womanliness" of the students:

> Woman's power in society and the family is certainly on the increase, due, I think, to her increased intelligence. Hence we feel that in Christianizing the women we are Christianizing the men, and when God rules in the hearts of the wives and mothers of these households it will make but little difference who occupies the throne. [15]

The reports coming out of Japan would have affirmed the women who read them: first, in the importance of their own roles as wives and mothers, and second, in the importance of their support of the Christian education of girls and women who would be or already were fulfilling these important roles in society. But the progress being made in Japan could not be found in India and China where the RCA was also engaged in education work with women. In these countries there was greater resistance to female education in general, and Christian education in particular. Thus, the pages of the *Gleaner* rarely include reports of rejoicing in the virtues and power of Christian women in India and China.

13. The *Mission Gleaner* 3, no. 4 (1886): 5-6.
14. The *Mission Gleaner* 1, no. 5 (July/August 1884): 7.
15. The *Mission Gleaner* 10, no. 6 (September/October 1893): 9-10.

What the female missionaries did report concerning India and China was the powerlessness and poverty of women in these societies. They saw the ways that the male society oppressed them. Many who became Christian were persecuted, and some were thrown out of their households and deprived of the opportunity to exercise their spiritual powers as wives and mothers. Although the harsh realities of women's lives in India and China made it difficult to find examples to support the ideal of the spiritually powerful Victorian woman, the ideal continued to be an important factor motivating women's missionary work to women. In fact, it was the dark side of women's power in China which caused one male writer to insist that, "Until the women are reached, nothing can be considered as permanently accomplished. It is they who teach the nation to be idolatrous, training the children in superstition from the very dawn of reason." [16]

The *Gleaner* further reinforced the Victorian ideal concerning girls and women through the telling of endless stories which confirmed that girls and women possess the power to change the hearts of evil men, whether they be American or foreign-born. One little Japanese girl who heard the story of Noah told it to her drunken father. At first he laughed at her, but then he took up the Bible himself, began going to church, and eventually was baptized. He became the church's most liberal supporter.[17] In a similar story, a fifteen-year-old girl "who gave her heart to Jesus" urged her drunken father to also believe. He persecuted her but finally believed and became an elder in the church.[18] A seven-year-old girl in the United States was on her death bed and called her pastor in. To him she gave all of her savings, four dollars and a few cents, to build a church for the poor. She died. When the pastor told her story from the pulpit, there were "tears in every eye," and then, "one wealthy man after another came forward with his offering." That church was built on the little girl's virtue.[19]

Not all of the exemplary stories are about girls; some demonstrate the spiritual influence of mothers. My favorite is the story of eighteen-year-old Maggie who is coming to terms with the true meaning of Christmas and God's precious gift to her. On Christmas Day, after much inner struggling, Maggie gives herself as a gift to Jesus and turning to her dear mother says,

16. The *Mission Gleaner* 1, no. 4 (1884): 5-6.
17. The *Mission Gleaner* 10, no. 2 (January/February 1893): 5.
18. The *Mission Gleaner* 2, no. 4 (May/June 1885): 6.
19. The *Mission Gleaner* 3, no. 6 (September/October 1886): 11.

"You can let me go somewhere, anywhere where they do not know of God's Christmas gift." As Maggie began to think of her future as a missionary, her mother "remembered the Christmas Day eighteen years ago, when she had given up her first born for the glory of His name, and knew that her gift had been accepted." [20]

These stories and others like them send the message that girls and women, mothers and wives have a remarkable capacity to influence others for the good if only they will take their responsibilities seriously. Most of the men who appear in these stories are the epitome of evil. Apart from a few rare exceptions, boys are usually depicted as unruly creatures who upon hearing the stories of "heathen" children covet their wild lives and freedom from going to school.[21] It is impossible to determine the impact of these stories. We cannot discover how they shaped the self-perceptions of their readers. But the intent is clear—to communicate that girls and women are the gentlest and most spiritually empowered creatures on the face of the earth, the most potent source for the reform of men and society. It was up to mothers and wives to see that this spiritual and moral power would be present in the next generation so that they could carry on the urgent work of Christ's mission.

Actually the publishers of the *Gleaner*, the woman's board, needed more from these women than their faithful service as wives and mothers. They needed them to be well informed about the church's missions. They needed their money. They needed their time. They needed their leadership on behalf of other church women, boys, and girls. How did they motivate the women to read more, to care more, and to give more? As we have seen, the *Gleaner* constantly referred women back to the call of the gospel and the "Great Commission" given to them on Easter morning. It also lifted up the Victorian ideal of true womanhood, which reinforced the conviction that the fate of the whole world depended on the conversion of women to Christianity, and that this effort depended especially on the women of the church.

In addition, the *Gleaner* constantly called the women to ever greater sacrifice and self-denial for the sake of missions. Women were urged to give up some of their luxuries, to forego the purchase of new parlor furniture, to wear last summer's clothes in order to give to the support of the missionary

20. The *Mission Gleaner* 11, no. 7 (November/December 1894): 16-19.
21. The *Mission Gleaner* 11, no. 1 (November/December 1893): 18-19.

women who had given up so much to relieve the suffering of the women of China, India, and Japan. Here there was some tension for the church's women. They needed certain things in order to maintain a proper home. Now they were being asked to give a portion of their household budget to the work of missions, to make sacrifices and to work "till you make happy every home in the world."[22]

Cultivating Leaders at Home

At the local level, leaders were essential to the task of keeping women aware and showing the way to greater sacrifice. This brings us to the third area of focus: the successes and frustrations the women encountered in their attempts to find leaders, to organize and raise support on the homefront. The women's board depended on women's auxiliaries at the local level to help raise awareness and money. The *Mission Gleaner* played an important role in encouraging women's leadership, providing materials for women's and children's mission meetings, and keeping all of the church's women informed of the activities of the various auxiliaries and the substance of classical union meetings.

One can conclude from reading the *Gleaner* that it was not always easy to find women willing to assume leadership for a woman's auxiliary or a children's mission society. The magazine offered a possible scenario for how to begin an organization and enthusiastic encouragement for anyone brave enough to step forward. Two women in a church might accept the responsibility, then,

> With consent of the pastor, they go forward, modestly, a call is made; it needs but this spark applied, hearts kindle...a quiet and systematic work is organized.... The result is that for several years, hundreds of dollars are sent to the treasuries of our Boards. Do not fear then to lead off, the beginning once made, there is no fear of failure.[23]

Simple as this sounds, apparently women were not leaping up to lead. Convinced that there were plenty of competent women who could offer

22. The *Mission Gleaner* 10, no. 2 (January/February 1893): 16.
23. The *Mission Gleaner* 1, no. 6 (September/October 1884): 3.

leadership, one writer speculated on why they didn't get to work. She concluded that,

> "One great reason is undue humility on the part of those who would and could [lead], and who shrink back lest they be deemed self-seeking for prominence. Thus the impulse to help in the good work is smothered, the band of workers not led on to service, and that church is a deserter from the ranks of the Lord's army."[24]

Perhaps the mention of these dire consequences was sufficient to relieve some women of their "undue humility" and to make them brave to lead. But the lack of leadership apparently continued, causing another writer to speculate that there were probably multiple reasons. Among them she cites apathy, lack of special education (perhaps the fault of the pastors), and a want of spiritual consecration.[25] These reasons are rather more serious than "undue humility." They point to the perception that there was a sad malaise among the church's women concerning mission.

Interestingly, the writers of the *Gleaner* stopped trying to figure out why women weren't leading and getting involved in the work of mission and instead began to focus more and more on providing resources to help those who were leading. The magazine was filled with helpful, practical instructions about how to organize and what to do at meetings. As reports from the various auxiliaries and children's mission societies came in to be printed in the column "Our Busy Women," it became clear that the women were listening to each other. Their meetings showed a remarkable uniformity from Grand Rapids to New Brunswick. Certain ideas spread like wildfire. "Envelope parties" were at the top of the hit parade. Each woman brought an envelope containing money, and either a prayer, an inspirational quotation, a scripture reading, a letter, or thanksgiving for mercies offered — something which would be read aloud by the leader. Apparently these meetings were very moving for the women.[26] Over time, the *Gleaner* also began providing thematic outlines for Bible studies. Every year, several new auxiliaries and children's societies were formed and celebrated in the *Gleaner*.

As the *Gleaner* tells it, a major accomplishment of the women's auxiliaries and the girl's mission societies was to allow and encourage women and girls

24. The *Mission Gleaner* 1, no. 6 (September/October 1884): 2.
25. The *Mission Gleaner* 4, no. 3 (March/April 1887): 4-6.
26. The *Mission Gleaner* 1, no. 6 (September/October 1984): 4.

to pray aloud in public. Usually, it was the responsibility of the leader to pray at the meetings. But when the women's board urged the auxiliaries to hold a prayer meeting, all the women were expected to pray. The women of Bethany Reformed, Grand Rapids, wrote about their experience:

> This was something unusual to us as a society, and as can be imagined looked forward to with a secret dread so well experienced by those who have never yet raised their voices in public prayer. But the call had come to us from our Master, and we could not refuse. Tongues were loosened.... We received such a blessing in remembering our brethren and sisters still in heathen darkness, as can only be received when we forget self in our Christian sympathy for others.[27]

In order to encourage the leaders of girls' groups to teach them to pray in public, one woman shared her technique. First she had the girls reciting Bible verses, poetry, and making reports. Then she asked them to come prepared to pray just a one sentence prayer at the next meeting. The girls admitted, "Our hearts were none too brave when we thought of praying aloud, even one sentence, before each other. How could we feel otherwise when we had never let anyone but our mothers hear our prayers."[28] Eventually, they did it and were surprised to see it was really an easy thing to pray aloud. These little mission bands were nurturing a new generation of female leaders for the church.

The *Gleaner* shows that the women's success in raising up the girls was offset by a major struggle to find ways of organizing and involving the boys in the work of missions. Women lamented the lack of interest in missions on the part of boys and men. They expressed deep concern about whether they would be able to raise up the next generation of male missionaries. Over and over the call went out from the *Gleaner* for any and all help in enlisting boys in the cause of missions. Women who had succeeded in the task shared their observations and strategies. Writes one woman, "Whoever undertakes this will not, I hope, make the mistake of thinking it will be the same kind of a charge as that of little girls, or that it is smooth and easy work. Boys are boys, in a missionary society as well as in school, or at play."[29] In spite of this sage

27. The *Mission Gleaner* 11, no. 6 (September/October 1894): 14.
28. The *Mission Gleaner* 3, no. 5 (July/August 1986): 10.
29. The *Mission Gleaner* 3, no. 6 (September/October 1886): 7.

advice, some women reported teaching the boys to sew just as they taught the girls in mission societies.[30] Others resisted the temptation of having boys behave like girls and found more suitable work for them to do, like making scrapbooks, sanding, painting, and making wooden tops.[31]

It was assumed that even older boys wanted to work for missions, and would work, if only a woman were willing to lead them. A story about a fifteen-year-old boy named Malcolm exemplified this fact.[32] Feeling slighted that there were organizations for "King's Daughters," but none for "Kings Sons," he begged his "dear, sweet, little mother" to lead him and his friends. Of course she agreed immediately. He gathered his friends together and "in humble imitation of the 'favored sex' they began by sending a box to the West" full of magazines and books. This pious mother was allowed only to superintend while the boys did this "men's work" of packing the box. Another woman reported success working with older boys by forming Missionary Literary Societies or Debating Clubs "conducted according to Parliamentary usage." "They run Parliamentary usage into the ground," she wrote. "Why they even call me to order."[33] Older girls were encouraged to bring boys and young men to Christian Endeavor Mission Meetings. They were instructed to "pray about it, work for it; not that they may fall in love with you, but with your Master."[34] In the years of the *Gleaner* which I have studied, the problem of what to do with the boys was not solved. But there are other successes praised on its pages.

Through the reports of women's classical meetings and anniversary meetings of the women's board, it becomes evident that the women were increasingly confident in their ability to maintain their own mission affairs. Most of these meetings followed a predictable pattern. The pastor of the church in which they were meeting would open with prayer and devotions. Then, church auxiliaries' reports were followed by the presentation of papers, usually by women, sometimes by female missionaries. They spoke on topics such as "Medical Missions: the Ministry of Woman to her Sex in Heathen Lands," "God's Method of Evangelizing the World," "Educational Work for Women," and typically, there was a presentation concerning domestic missions. From the morning session the women would adjourn to

30. The *Mission Gleaner* 2, no. 1 (November/December 1884): 2.
31. The *Mission Gleaner* 5, no. 5 (July/August 1888): 8-9.
32. The *Mission Gleaner* 12, no. 6 (September/October 1895): 14-15.
33. The *Mission Gleaner* 5, no. 5 (July/August 1888): 8-9.
34. The *Mission Gleaner* 10, no. 2 (January/February 1893): 17.

a "delightful" lunch prepared by the women of the church, and a time of "sweet" fellowship. Afternoon sessions often included presentations by ministers, male missionaries, and/or members of the mens' board. Following these formal presentations, the "Question Box," which contained questions written by the women was opened, and their questions answered by those who had provided leadership for the day, or by others who might have the expertise to answer. Then there was the singing of a final hymn, and the pronouncing of the benediction by the pastor of the church.[35]

The record shows that these meetings were attended mostly by "enthusiastic" women, but sometimes one could find "an agreeable sprinkling of grave divines and sympathetic laymen,"[36] or "a few gentlemen [who] had the courage to be present."[37] But, every now and again, the women insisted on and delighted in having meetings in which the men were entirely excluded from the leadership. The first report of such a meeting appeared in 1885 and described the aim of a meeting led entirely by women as follows: "It was hoped that thus there might be increased freedom in discussion and enlarged opportunity for a mutual interchange of thought and experiences among its members. It was generally admitted that the change was a marked advantage over previous methods."[38] A similar report appeared in 1887. The female reporter for the 1895 anniversary of the women's board rejoiced in the fact that the meeting was "quite emphatically a 'women's meeting.'" So as not to appear too insubordinate, she goes on to say, "Not that we wished to shove the men out into the cold... — perish the thought! for we could not do without them; but when there are women, able and willing to speak, and with a direct message from women to women, let us hear them."[39]

The *Mission Gleaner* reveals that women in the Reformed church were searching for and finding their own voice and place in the church's leadership. They needed a space which was entirely their own in order to develop their voice and to gain confidence in their ability to lead within the sphere assigned them. Of course, when there were no men allowed, and therefore no pastors, the women's meetings could not end with the benediction. Instead the women sang the doxology and went on their way. But perhaps

35. See for example the *Mission Gleaner* 11, no. 1 (November/December 1884): 1-2; 11, no. 1 (November/December 1885): 4.
36. The *Mission Gleaner* 3, no. 4 (May/June 1886): 1.
37. The *Mission Gleaner* 7, no. 1 (November/December 1889): 4.
38. The *Mission Gleaner* 3, no. 1 (November/December 1885): 1.
39. The *Mission Gleaner* 12, no. 5 (July/August 1895): 3.

even on those occasions they did not go without the benediction. In a memorial tribute for Mrs. Sturges, president of the women's board for nearly twenty years, we read, "It was a great privilege to have her in our meetings, for her presence was a benediction."[40] Perhaps the *Gleaner* was an important resource in confirming for the women that, like Abraham, they had been blessed by God to be a blessing, to one another, and to their sisters on the other side of the world.

On the pages of the *Mission Gleaner* I find the story of Reformed church women committing themselves to the work of raising up women on the other side of the world and in their own midst. In many ways, the *Gleaner* served to reinforce their traditional roles as wives and mothers, although it was hoped that their domestic efforts would be redirected toward goals of mission. But the *Gleaner* also tells the story of women finding their own voices and claiming new roles as competent leaders in the ministry and mission of the church. Perhaps through this telling, the *Mission Gleaner* encouraged more and more girls and women to find their voices and to trust that Christ might be commissioning them to lead and share the gospel story, just as he had commissioned Mary on that very first Easter morning.

40. The *Mission Gleaner* 11, no. 6 (September/October 1894): 1.

IX

The Education of Miss Sara Couch:
The Preparation of Women for Foreign Missionary Service in the Reformed Church in American in the Late Nineteenth Century

Jennifer Mary Reece

"To love them and suffer with them."

In the autumn of 1892, an unmarried twenty-five-year-old schoolteacher from New York State embarked in San Francisco on a steamer bound for Japan, arriving in the bustling port city of Nagasaki in late October. Sara Maria Couch would live and work in Nagasaki as a missionary for the Reformed Church in America (RCA) for the next half century and more. Her official retirement came in 1937, yet even then she chose not to return to the United States but instead to continue her life and work in partnership with a Japanese woman, her former student, Tomegawa Jun. When, as World War II threatened, most other Western missionaries left Japan, Sara Couch stayed on in Nagasaki. "Where would I go? What would I do?" she asked in a letter. "Japan is my home now, for better or for worse."[1]

---

1. Sara M. Couch, Nagasaki, to Luman J. Shafer (secretary, Board of Foreign Missions, RCA), New York, undated letter, Japan Mission File (1941), RCA Archives, Gardner Sage Library, New Brunswick Theological Seminary, New Brunswick, New Jersey.

Late in 1941, when she was seventy-four, Sara Couch was arrested by the Japanese and interned for the duration of the war, first in a school building in Nagasaki, and then in a camp in Tokyo. On her release four years later she found, much to her relief, that Tomegawa Jun had survived, and that their home had remained standing, protected by a hillside from the worst of the blast of the atomic bomb dropped on Nagasaki by the United States. Their rooms were filled with broken glass: "all our goods are in a mixed-up mess," she wrote. Worse in that devastated city, "we do not yet know the fate of many of our friends." She assured her U.S. friends that even now she had no thought of leaving: "I am back in Nagasaki and plan to stay, if the Lord permits."[2] Permission was granted, it seems: when Sara Couch died the following January, two weeks after her seventy-ninth birthday, Tomegawa Jun buried her not in the international cemetery in Nagasaki, but in the Japanese one. Here too, in 1974, Tomegawa Jun would herself be buried beside the American woman with whom she had lived and worked most of her adult life, their graves marked with a single stone.[3] In one of her last letters from bombed-out Nagasaki, Sara Couch had summed up, in her characteristically quiet way, the whole of her missionary theology and practice: "Beyond praying, I believe just now the most I can do for the people of this city is to love them and suffer with them."[4]

What had prepared this missionary to live out such a theology — simple, yet profound — of love for and suffering with the neighbor? What education had enabled Sara, and other women like her, to move half-way across the world to become the teacher, and the faithful friend, of women and girls in a culture vastly different from her own? What training had she received that gave her not only the skills for mission work but also the strength for such an extended term of service? How typical was her experience? The tale of the education of Miss Sara Couch, set against the stories of some of the other women who offered themselves for mission service to the Reformed Church in America at the end of the nineteenth century, may provide some answers and may also yield insight into the developments in education, gender roles,

2. Sara M. Couch, Nagasaki, to Luman J. Shafer, New York, November, 1945, Japan Mission File (1945), RCA Archives.
3. Lane R. Earns, "At Home with a Friend: The Story of Sara Couch and Tomegawa Jun," *Crossroads: A Journal of Nagasaki History and Culture* 1:1 (Summer 1993): 47, 57-58.
4. Sara M. Couch, Nagasaki, to Emma Kollen Pieters [U.S.A.], 5 October, 1945, Japan Mission File (1945), RCA Archives.

and cross cultural experience which were changing the religious life of American women a hundred years ago.

The life and work of Sara Couch in Japan was first brought to my attention a decade ago by the archivist of the Reformed Church in America, Russell Gasero, in an article published in *Historical Highlights*, an occasional publication of the Historical Society of the RCA.[5] Sara Couch's career was almost exactly contemporaneous with the "heyday" of the foreign missionary movement (1880-1930) and therefore can illuminate women's participation in it, until recently a neglected area of mission history.[6] The focus of this essay is limited to one aspect of female missionary careers: education and preparation for missionary service. Sixty-five applications of female missionary candidates to the Board of Foreign Missions of the RCA have been studied to help determine how typical Sara Couch was in training and background. The bulk of these applications were made between 1880 and 1910; some from an earlier period (1860-1879) will be used for historical comparison. These papers reveal sometimes a wealth of information, and sometimes only tantalizing hints about the applicants' family backgrounds, general education,

5. Russell L. Gasero, "Out of the Stacks: Sara Couch, 1867-1946," *Historical Highlights: The Journal of Reformed Church History* 6:3 (September, 1985): 3-11. My thanks to him for much help, and for his dedicated work in preserving and providing access to the important historical records of the RCA. I am also grateful to Library Director Renée House — and the staff of the Gardner Sage Library; to Dr. John W. Coakley, L. Russell Feakes Memorial Professor of Church History at New Brunswick Theological Seminary; to Professor James Moorhead and my colleagues in the American Church History Graduate Seminar of Princeton Theological Seminary (1994-95) for comments on early drafts of this material; and to participants in the Standing Seminar on Reformed Church History (especially Dr. John Beardslee and Rev. Lewis Scudder) for helping me to clarify some of the issues. Further results of my research into the life of Sara M. Couch can be found in Una Ratmeyer's *Hands, Hearts, and Voices: Women Who Followed God's Call*, (New York:1995), pp. 22-24. The only other published material on Sara Couch is that of Dr. Lane Earns of the University of Wisconsin, historian of Nagasaki, whom I thank for his generous sharing of his research.
6. See William Hutchison, *Errand to the World: American Protestant Thought and Foreign Missions*, (Chicago and London: 1987; pbk ed., 1993), p. 1. Recent works providing a gender analysis of the missionary movement include: Virginia Hill, *The World Their Household: The American Woman's Foreign Mission Movement and Cultural Transformation: 1870-1920*, (Ann Arbor: 1985); Jane Hunter, *The Gospel of Gentility: American Women Missionaries in Turn-of-the-century China*, (New Haven, 1984) and Dana Robert, *American Women in Mission: a Social History of their Thought and Practice*, (Macon, Ga. 1996).

work experiences, physical health and spiritual life that propelled them into the loving and suffering lives of missionary women.

Farmers' daughters at home

In both her initial application to the Board of Foreign Missions and her later reports back to the United States, Sara Couch is extremely reticent about her personal life and family background. Hints about her early vocation must be gleaned from census data and other public records, as well as from denominational sources.[7] She was born in the village of Schoharie in rural upstate New York in January, 1867. The civil war was over, and there was a surge of optimism and growth, in the North at least.[8] Sara's grandfather, one Charles Couch, had taken part in the great westward expansion of the young republic, moving to New York State from Connecticut, first to Dutchess County and then, in 1832, west again, across the Hudson into Schoharie County, with his son Smith and daughter Mariah. There they farmed almost 200 of the pleasant farm land watered by the Schoharie creek. A mixed-farming enterprise typical of its time, the holding included a small flock of sheep, some pigs and chickens, and a couple of dairy cows, along with the crops: oats, buckwheat, corn, hay, and root vegetables.

In the New York State Census of 1855, Sara Couch's father, Smith B. Couch, is listed as a married man, dwelling with an extended family: his widowed father, Charles Couch Sr.; his young son, Charles Couch II; his maiden sister, Mariah Couch; a boarder, Alanson Eaton, who worked as a farm laborer; and Alanson's sister Lydia Anne, who is listed as a "domestic." This live-in servant became his second wife sometime in the 1860s. In 1866 they had a son, Lee, and in 1867, a daughter, whom they named Sara Maria. The aunt for whom she was named, Mariah Couch, surely provided for the

---

7. The New York Census for 1855, 1865, and 1875 provided minute details concerning the inhabitants of Schoharie County. The U.S. Census of 1885 was less helpful in locating specific persons. Birth and death records were obtained from the "Vital Statistics Index," New York State Archives, State Library, Albany, N.Y. Further information was provided by issues of a Schoharie County newspaper, the *Canojoharie Index* 1882-1883 and 1889-1890, New York State Library, Albany, N. Y.
8. John H. Houck of Central Bridge, N. Y., the census taker for Schoharie County in 1865, noted "stimulous in business of all kinds. The Farmer, Mechanic, Lawyer, Doctor, and Laborer [....] are in one grand charge of conquest, and with a zeal never before witnessed." New York State, *Census*, 1865. New York State Archives, State Library, Albany, N. Y.

young Sara Couch a role model of an unmarried woman exercising a certain amount of independence within the confines of the family structure: Mariah is listed in the census records as actually owning much of the land farmed by the family.[9] The Couch family was not large by Victorian standards, but in 1875 the farmhouse was comfortably filled by Smith and Lydia, Smith's son Charles, unmarried sister Mariah, an elderly relative, Mary Wright, and the two children, Lee and Sara. In a decade this would all change.

Again, the census and other public records tell the story to which Sara Couch herself referred only obliquely in later years. In 1882, when she was fifteen, her father died at age seventy, probably of heart disease (he had been subject to "rheumatics" during his life). In September, 1888, Mary Wright, the old lady who had been cared for in the family home, died, but more unexpected losses followed. In January of 1890, during one of the harshest winters in memory, Lee Couch died of pneumonia, aged twenty-four; finally, in October of the same year, Lydia Ann Eaton Couch died of unrecorded causes. Sara Couch was orphaned; the once bustling farmhouse now housed only the two bachelors, both much older than herself. She applied to the Board of Foreign Missions just over a year later, in January of 1892.

Sara Couch's tragedy-filled young life fits into a model that many nineteenth-century missionary women shared. It has been shown that severe personal family loss was quite common as a catalyst for women to enter the missionary field—especially if they were single.[10] Overwhelmingly, female missionaries were women with some education who came from working—though not poor—backgrounds, much more often rural than urban. Farmers' daughters, they often had received some teacher training at the local Normal School and some years' teaching in the primary grades, and they were feeling a need for larger horizons. However, there were as yet

9. Sara's father owned only 80 acres of it himself in 1875, while Mariah Couch owned over 160 acres, including all the farm buildings except for the dwelling house. At his death, Smith B. Couch seems to have owned the whole of the Couch farm. I have not yet located a death record or will for Mariah Couch. It has been suggested to me that her ownership of the property during her lifetime may have been a family arrangement made for tax purposes.

10. Hunter, pp. 40-42. The proportion of orphaned women in her study is high: "Of those in the American Board whose family circumstances at the time of departure are known, 17 percent were without both parents and 51 percent without one" (p.40). It is unclear, however, how this compares with statistics for the general population.

few other opportunities for women. Such women, if they were at all religious, were apt to be drawn toward the missionary work portrayed so heroically in the many women's missionary journals such as the Reformed Church's *Mission Gleaner*. Often coming from the Midwest of the United States, they were unlikely to have traveled far beyond their small towns or to have seen many cultures outside of their own quite circumscribed surroundings.[11] These characteristics seem to hold true for female applicants to the Reformed Church Board of Foreign Missions: those from small town and rural communities outnumbered women from urban areas in a ratio of over two to one. Complete family information was not available for all the women studied, but fifteen out of thirty-two had experienced the death of mother or father, or both, or had experienced other significant family losses.[12] Much of the work of Sara Couch in Japan was centered around creating a home, a Christian home, for the Japanese girls in Sturges Seminary, for the small Christian Protestant community in Nagasaki, and for Tomegawa Jun. As for many other single women missionaries, her early loss of a home and family was transformed in a foreign land where she learned how to be, as Lane Earns has put it, "at home with a friend."[13]

"Faith in the God of truth and love"

Some kind of spiritual formation has usually been a part of missionary preparation. Candidates for the mission field in the Reformed Church in America in the nineteenth century were required to give proof of their membership in a church by means of a testimonial from their pastor and "from persons of intelligence and piety" who could attest "to his Christian character and standing as a member of the Church."[14] The board admitted

11. Ibid., pp. 28-29.
12. Applicant Files, Board of Foreign Missions, RCA Archives. Thirty seven (37) women studied came from rural or small town environments; seventeen (17) came from urban centers (counting Grand Rapids, Michigan, as "urban"); the origins of eleven (11) were unknown or outside of North America. That they came from the East (33) more than from the Midwest (21) had much to do with the demographics of the RCA in the nineteenth century.
13. Lane Earns, article title, p.47, et passim. He depicts Tomegawa Jun as also suffering early tragedy, her mother and sister dying before she was four years old; much later Tomegawa would refer to Sara Couch, eighteen years her senior, as someone she "learned to love as a mother." Lane Earns, pp. 50-51.
14. Board of Foreign Missions RCA, *Manual of the Board... For the Use of Missionary Candidates....* (New York, 1885), p. 5.

that their specifications were very general; they "do not differ materially from those which would render a minister or other Christian worker useful and acceptable at home. They are such as these—devoted and consistent piety and consecration to Christ and His glory...."[15] The applicants and their sponsors also tended to speak in very general terms about their faith, if they mentioned it at all. Sara Couch is one who almost completely failed to mention her faith in a personal way during the application process. A letter from the pastor in the Schoharie church gave a brief indication that she was a member in good standing. She had been confirmed as a member of the Reformed Church in Schoharie in 1883 — the year following the death of her father. In 1884, the report of the Classis of Schoharie to the Synod of Albany celebrates "a blessed revival of religion" in the area for the previous year, remarking with satisfaction that "the prominence of Sabbath School work... is marked and inspiring."[16] During these years Schoharie and other places on the edges of the old "burned-over" district of upstate New York[17] were once again drawing the attention of evangelists, most notably Dwight Lyman Moody. In 1890, for example, he and the very popular Ira Sankey were the big draw for the "fifth annual convention of Christian Endeavor Societies of New York and New Jersey." As many as 2,500 young people attended this three-day conference in Rochester. In the following month of the same year, the Synod of Albany (RCA) held a missionary conference in Albany.[18]

Whether Sara Couch attended such conferences or not, they were part of the atmosphere of excitement in Protestant North America, whose increasing wealth and industrialization were awakening a social conscience. Was it not the duty of prosperous Americans, went the message, to carry the gospel of

15. Ibid., p. 3.
16. Particular Synod of Albany, RCA, *Minutes*: 1884, p. 15; 1885, p.47. Archives of the RCA.
17. "Burned-over" refers to the many revivals that ran like wildfire through the western part of New York State in the nineteenth century. "Defined by the route of the Erie Canal, the Burned-over District extended from just east of Utica to just west of Buffalo, north to the foothills of the Adirondacks and the shore of Lake Ontario, and south to the tip of the Finger Lakes, according to Michael Barkun, *Crucible of the Millennium: The Burned-Over District of New York in the 1840s* (Syracuse, 1986),p. 3. By this definition, the Schoharie valley is outside of the burned-over district, southeast of Utica. But the revival ferment had penetrated, by the latter decades of the nineteenth century, even the historically antirevival Dutch Reformed dominated areas of the state like Albany and Schenectady, especially since the 1859 "Fulton Street Revival."
18. Particular Synod of Albany, *Minutes*: 1891, p. 18.

Christ, and the good news of the progress of civilization, to the "heathen" world? Dwight Lyman Moody was especially fervent in his appeals to his hearers that they waste no time in reaching the "unsaved": to him the world was a giant shipwreck, and Western Protestant Christianity was the lifeboat. "If you have any friends on this wreck unsaved," warned the evangelist, "you had better lose no time in getting them off."[19] Moody and other pre-millennial preachers were convinced that the second coming of Jesus was imminent and that Christians must work furiously to save as many souls as possible. "Rescue the perishing!" sang the congregations he inspired, and they signed up in droves to do it. The theologies of these rescue workers ranged over a wide spectrum, from pre-millennial evangelists like Moody to post-millennial advocates of a "social gospel," such as the best-selling author, Josiah Strong. Many shared his belief that God had appointed to Western Protestantism a starring role in the drama of salvation: that of the chosen hero laboring mightily at the oars of civilization in order to carry the hope of life in Christ to the sinking world.[20]

Influential and inspiring as the evangelical message was for many missionaries, not all of them shared either Moody's pre-millennial theology or Strong's conviction of Anglo-Saxon cultural superiority. Sara Couch's writings show her piety to be much different: neither dogmatic nor aggressive. She rarely talks about "the heathen" except very occasionally in the description of a specific Buddhist or Shinto religious ritual. When she speaks of the people of Nagasaki it is always in terms of family and neighborhood: "We earnestly pray that the house may be a blessing not only to us who live in it but to all who live about us and all who enter its doors. Our work takes us all over the city, but one great desire of our hearts is to find ways to help our neighbors."[21] Her expressions of piety are also often couched in familial language: God as Father is for her a metaphor not expressing distant authority but an intimate and personal relationship which directs and makes sense of the small details as well as the grand plan of her life. Her commitment to membership in the Schoharie church in the year after her own father died and her decision to serve as a missionary after the destruction

19. Dwight L. Moody, *New Sermons* (New York, 1880), p. 535.
20. See Josiah Strong, *Our Country* (New York, 1886) and *The New Era, or, The Coming Kingdom* (New York, 1893). Both books appeared in multiple editions over several decades.
21. Sara Couch, "Evangelistic work: Nagasaki," Women's Board of Foreign Missions (WBFM), RCA, *Annual Report* 59 (1929), p. 51.

of her family of origin suggest that her faith provided her with a new sense of family and of purpose. The family could stretch to include the Japanese girls at Sturges Seminary in Nagasaki, with whom Sara Couch said she "felt at home" as soon as she arrived.[22] It could stretch to include the children in the poorest neighborhoods of Nagasaki, as well as the men and women from the former *samurai* class of Japan, who were becoming converted to Christianity.

Her faith not only stretched the bounds of her definition of family but helped her and others endure the otherwise unendurable. Lois Kramer, another missionary who was interned for a time by the Japanese in the 1940s, bore witness to the deep roots of the faith with which Miss Couch inspired the other detainees: "After we were burned out she read me a quotation which she had written in her Bible many years ago. 'We can afford to lose anything & everything except faith in the God of truth and love.'"[23] One can speculate that Sara Couch had penned those words when, newly orphaned, she discovered new life and purpose through exploring the faith in which she had been baptized and raised.

"A Scholar, a Lady, and a Christian"

When the formal education of Sara Couch is considered, we may note that her training illustrates a turning point for the education of female missionaries in the late nineteenth century, and indeed of the education of women in general. After graduating from the village schools of Schoharie, Sara Couch enrolled in 1885 at the Normal School in Albany, New York, for training as a teacher. In September of 1888 she began work as a teacher in the primary department of the Mechanicville, New York, Union School. After her second year of teaching in Mechanicville, with her mother recently dead and her elder brother Charles contemplating a move westward to Superior, Wisconsin, Sara applied to the Moody Bible School in Chicago, Illinois, for training as a missionary. Her missionary course lasted for one academic year (fall of 1891 to summer of 1892), in the course of which she applied to her

---

22. Sara Couch, *Mission Gleaner* 10:1 (November-December, 1892): 11.
23. Lois F. Kramer, Evangelical Mission, Tokyo, to Luman J. Shafer, New York, 3 September, 1945. Japan Mission File (1945) RCA Archives.

denomination for appointment as a missionary, suggesting that God's call to serve would find her willing to go "as far as Africa." She received her assignment in May of 1892, to Japan.[24]

In 1885, as Sara Couch entered Albany Normal School (the institution which formed the nucleus of what is now the State University of New York at Albany), she represented the growing edge of a movement for higher education for women which was at the same time popular and still quite controversial. Teaching had by this date become a profession which gave women standing and prestige in the community; this was increased by the opening of special training schools for teachers, called normal schools because they were designed to raise the level of education in the common and village schools all over the country to a coherent set of standards or norms. Young women were especially eager to attend these schools, which brought post-secondary education into reach for women who could not aspire to the few colleges open to women.[25] Twelve of the female applicants in this study experienced some normal school training. One of them, Mary Deyo, also a single woman sent to Japan, reported with some pride in her application that, "on the opening of the Normal School at New Paltz I entered that institution, in March 1886, and was graduated from there last June," going on to say that she had returned there after graduation as a teacher herself. This was by no means an unusual path for a good student to take.[26]

24. Her suggestion about Africa is odd, as the RCA had no mission in Africa at this time. This, and the fact that she is obviously surprised to find out about the existence of the Women's Board of Foreign Missions (organized in 1875), suggests that her denominational ties were quite loose. This seems typical of many missionaries of the RCA. A surprising proportion of the women studied here whose denominational background could be ascertained came from outside the RCA: 16 out of 65, or almost 25 percent. They were Presbyterians, Methodist, Baptists, Congregationalists and Episcopalians.
25. Barbara Solomon, *In the Company of Educated Women*, (New Haven, 1985) p. 20; see also Helen L. Horowitz, *Alma Mater: Design and Experience in the Women's Colleges from Their NineteenthCentury Beginnings to the 1930s*, (New York, 1984).
26. Despite this training and experience, Mary Deyo showed little confidence in herself as a teacher of religion, however: "correct religious instruction has always seemed to me to be of infinitely greater importance than any other teaching," she said in a later letter. "Of my own skill in imparting such instruction, however, I have great doubts." She in fact became one of the more successful missionaries to Japan, not as a teacher, but as an evangelist. Missionary Candidate Files, RCA Archives.

Such normal schools for teacher training were drawing more and more women students in part because girls who continued with schooling past the primary levels needed teachers. In the 1880s and 1890s, young women started to flock to public high schools, and education previously open only to the wealthy was now available to the growing mass of middle-class women. The extraordinary jump in the numbers of women who applied to the missionary fields in these decades is explained in part by this unprecedented level of education ordinary women were able to achieve. By 1900, women high school graduates outnumbered men in an astonishing two-to-one ratio and were outperforming men in almost every part of the curriculum.[27] Women with high school and college educations wanted a broader range of possibilities for their new skills and ambitions; at the same time, the demands of the mission field compelled women to get further training. The great majority of male missionaries were ordained pastors, which meant, for those in the Reformed church with its historic ideal of an educated clergy, education at a theological college. To be without any college education at all would have put a woman missionary at even more of a disadvantage than the mere fact of her gender. But what opportunity was there for women to gain a theological education?

Before the 1890s, theological training of any sort was almost impossible for most women. From the beginning, however, the movement for women's education in the United States had been linked to the idea that the minds, spirits, and bodies of young girls ought to receive a structured preparation for service to their families, to their communities, and to their God. Missionary service was the ideal which inspired many early educators to open colleges for girls and young women. From the applications of eleven women applying to the Board of Foreign Missions before 1880, we learn that four received an education at institutions with an explicit missionary purpose: the Elmira Female College in Elmira, New York, and Mount Holyoke Female Seminary in Massachusetts. Elmira College was formed in 1859 by an RCA pastor, the Rev. Samuel R. Brown, D.D., who with his wife, Elizabeth, and daughter Julia left soon after its incorporation to become one of the first North American missionary families to Japan.[28] Mary Lyon's

---

27 John L. Rury, *Education and Women's Work: Female Schooling and the Division of Labor in Urban America, 1870-1930*. (Albany, N.Y., 1991), pp. 2-3; 6-7.

28. Arie Brouwer claimed that Elmira was "the first institution of higher education for women in America," in *Reformed Church Roots* (New York, 1977), p.98, echoing Edward Tanjore Corwin, *A Manual of the Reformed Church in America*,

school at Mount Holyoke was founded, like Samuel Brown's, with the explicit purpose of cultivating young women who would live out her ideal of noble womanly service "in carrying the blessings of salvation to...the inhabitants of this benighted world to be converted to God through our instrumentality."[29] Another early candidate, Jane Zabriskie (later, Blauvelt), attended another, unnamed "female academy" in New Jersey. A teacher's letter of recommendation describes her as "most assiduous & successful, happily combining docility with independence of thought." Another teacher gushes, "Miss Zabriskie manifested more than ordinary maturity of mind and depth of thought..." while maintaining, "a delicate sense of propriety." In further recommendations from her teachers at the new Normal School of Trenton, she is lauded for her "high character as a Scholar, a Lady, and a Christian." The emphasis of the recommendation was distinctly on the last two terms. "Independence" of thought and expression was valued, so long as it was kept in check by "docility." Likewise, "depth" and "maturity" of thought were always to be tempered by "propriety."

By the end of the century, this kind of thinking was already beginning to seem old fashioned. Respectability was still valued, but the educated woman did not necessarily aspire to being a "lady." But the traditions emphasizing refined piety rather than scholarly accomplishment died hard, as is shown by the papers of another candidate who presented herself in the 1890s. Florence Bingham, in among the most engaging letters of the collection, described the sense of inadequacy she felt from her upper-class education at "The Misses' Robinsons" in New Jersey. She was well aware of the challenges, risks, and dangers she would face as a missionary: "separation, loneliness, homelessness, sickness, suffering, perhaps death, at foreign duty." In the face of these challenges, she wondered if her genteel learning and informal teaching experience in her own "kitchen school" had provided her with adequate preparation for missionary work, or whether she needed further training. "If a course of study is deemed necessary," she wrote,

1628-1902 (New York, 1902), 4th edition, p. 345. It may have been the first to give itself the exalted title "college," but it is doubtful that the course of instruction or the aims and goals differed much from those of Mount Holyoke (1836) or Emma Willard's school in Troy, N.Y. (1821).

29. Mary Lyon, "Principles and Design of the Mount Holyoke Female Seminary" (1837), in *Classics in the Education of Girls and Women*, Shirley Nelson Kersey, ed. (Metuchen, 1981), pp. 300-301.

"please tell me. I know so little of the 'how' to become a missionary though, thank God, I know now 'why' to become one." [30]

"How to become a missionary"

The road to missionary work for the majority of men in the RCA and other mainstream Protestant denominations was through the theological seminaries and the ordained ministry. As more and more women, especially single women, flocked to missionary work at the end of the century, few people suggested that women should be admitted to theological schools, or receive any special training other than as teachers or medical workers. The Victorian model of ideal womanhood included the assumption that women were by nature especially pious and religiously sensitive, making any special training unnecessary — especially for conveying the Christian faith to other women and to children.[31] Dwight Lyman Moody, so involved with the "why" of becoming a missionary, also stood out from the crowd in dedicating himself to solving the problem of "how" to prepare women for missionary service. Himself of uneducated background, D.L. Moody was a somewhat strange bed-fellow for the reverend doctors of the Reformed Church in America, and indeed he was viewed with suspicion by some. But his institute for female education at Northfield, where he also held annual summer conferences that attracted thousands from across the spectrum of young Protestant America, was warmly praised from the beginning, and Reformed church pastors and elders did not hesitate to send their daughters there to be educated and filled with missionary zeal.[32] It was at Northfield that Florence Bingham — and so many others — had discovered the "why" of missions. Of the fifty-four women in the later decades covered by this study (1881-1905), twelve can be associated directly with Moody either through Northfield Academy or the Moody Bible Institute (MBI) in Chicago, while

---

30. Florence Bingham, East Orange, New Jersey, to Henry Cobb (secretary of the Board of Foreign Missions, RCA), New York, 1 August, 1895, Missionary Candidate Files, RCA Archives.
31. Many works have described this. See especially: Ann Douglas, *The Feminization of American Culture*, (New York, 1978); Joan Jacobs Brumberg, *Mission For Life: The Story of the Family of Adoniram Judson, the Dramatic Effects of the First American Foreign Mission, and the Course of Evangelical Religion in the Nineteenth Century*, (New York, 1980); and the essays by Fabend, Gasero, and House in the present volume.
32. Virginia Brereton, *Training God's Army: American Bible Schools 1880-1940*, (Bloomington, 1990), p. 36.

a dozen more candidates mention Bible schools or missionary camps and conventions without specific names. Many of the files have descriptions such as the following from 1891:

> The thought of this [missionary life] has been on my heart and mind for more than a year, and this winter, while attending at Northfield, Mass, Mr. Moody's school for training Christian workers, the desire was greatly strengthened by the influences there and by the earnest talking of several missionaries who from time to time made addresses at the school.[33]

Some seminary-trained clergy tended to look down on the education that the women sought in such venues. The academic level of the Bible training institutes such as Moody's was certainly lower than that of most theological colleges. The historian Virginia Brereton draws a parallel between them and present day community or junior colleges, in that they filled a gap between high school and college education, had a strong focus on technical and practical work, and made explicit commitments to a non-elitist philosophy and to education as training for specific purposes rather than to learning for its own sake.[34]

The instruction at MBI was specifically geared to those people who were not served by existing theological colleges: working men, "second-career" men, laymen in general, and women. Moody liked to call all of them his "gap-men," meaning that they filled in a perceived cultural and class gap between the educated elite of the clergy and the "uncivilized heathens" who were the aim of missions. A kind of anticlerical, or at least lay-empowering, ethos was at the root of institutions like the MBI. The course of Bible study included some forays into original language training, but the emphasis was "inductive" study to unearth "the plain meaning of the text" and its application to "real life." The influence of science and technology on North American culture was evident in the attitude towards the Bible as a book full of literal prophecy and clear facts that could be learned systematically. Above all, the training at institutions like MBI stressed practical matters: to learn the nuts and bolts of street evangelism, women as well as men were sent on "visiting" tours around neighborhoods in Chicago as part of their education.[35]

33. Margaret Cumming Morrison, Bergen, N.J., to Henry Cobb, New York, [1891]: Missionary Candidate Files, RCA Archives.
34. Brereton, p. 35.
35. Ibid., pp. 58, 63, 80-81, 88-90.

Despite the difference between these schools and the RCA theological seminaries in New Jersey and Michigan, a candidate could hardly have a better reference than a course of study at the Moody Bible Institute, the YMCA-founded institute in Springfield, Massachusetts, or even at one of the local Bible training institutes that had sprung up like mushrooms in communities across the country from Albany to Kalamazoo and beyond. By the 1890s, as American society had become more urban, more professional, and more bureaucratic, a farm girl from a small valley in New York was able to find her way to the state capital and then to the big city to acquire the kind of practical education and training in specific skills that would commend her to her denominational board of foreign missions far more readily than the mere claim of an "ornamental" propriety, however pious. By bravely launching out into Chicago in 1892 for a course at the newly opened Moody Bible Institute, Sara Couch was riding the wave of the future and assuring herself of a welcome in the ever more professional milieu of missionary work. She was also taking one of the only avenues toward a theological education open to women.

"Education will make her rebellious"

The city of Nagasaki must have seemed to Sara Couch to offer the perfect opportunity to put into practice the city-evangelism techniques she had practiced in Chicago's neighborhoods while a student at MBI. As she was steaming to her destination, however, the needs of the RCA mission in Japan suddenly changed. Carrie Lanterman, beloved teacher at Sturges Seminary, a girls school begun in Nagasaki by members of the RCA mission, unexpectedly died. Sara Couch took her place as a teacher at the school, as a "temporary" replacement. This "temporary" arrangement was to last two decades, until 1913. Letters and reports at the time stress how compliant and amiable Sara Couch was in response to this change in plans, but there is also evidence that the substitution of teaching in a girls' school for the work of an evangelist in the city and outlying villages was not without hardship for the MBI-trained Sara Couch.

The tension between evangelization and education was felt by many women in the mission field. Touring the country villages or city neighborhoods, organizing clothing drives and food distribution, publishing newsletters, distributing Bibles and tracts, holding meetings for temperance and Bible study, addressing groups of adults and children in semi-public settings, and, later, giving "steropticon" and "magic lantern" presentations of the Christian faith — all this often seemed to be far more engaging and necessary work than teaching the children of upper-class Japanese a smattering of English and a touch of Western culture. Mission administrators tried hard to convince the field workers that the two kinds of work were not in conflict, and that "these two departments constantly overlap each other and are but different phases of the same work."[36] Missionary conferences continually debated this topic in the period between 1880 and 1900, suggesting an unresolved tension.[37]

The year 1913 found Sara Couch still at Sturges Seminary in Nagasaki, working as vice-principal under the leadership of the principal, a Mr. Hirotsu. For economic and social reasons the mission decided that it was no longer feasible to continue Sturges as a separate institution, and it was decided to merge with a Presbyterian girls' school to form a new seminary at Shimonoseki, 200 miles to the north of Nagasaki. The mission made its wishes known to Sara Couch: that she would make the move with the rest of the school. She refused, as quietly and politely as possible. But she handed the mission what amounted to an ultimatum. "Miss Couch sprang a surprise on us. She is contemplating asking for a two year leave of absence instead of a furlough, to be spent in Japan — there was some talk of it being without salary." In other words, if she was forced to go to Shimonoseki and continue with the school work, she would quit.[38]

Sara Couch's photographs from those days show a small, crumpled, rather mousy woman, not someone who might be expected to take a stand or even to stand up for herself. Her letters to the women's board always expressed a sense of humility about her work; but now it was combined with a kind of dogged determination to stay in Nagasaki:

> I am sure the ladies of the Board overestimate my work for it has always been very full of mistakes. I think perhaps the school has done more for me than I have done for the school. As I have

36. John G. Fagg, "Evangelism and Education," Address to the 25th annual meeting of the WBFM, *Annual Reports* 25(1899), p. 27.
37. See *Proceedings of the General Conference of Protestant Missionaries in Japan, Osaka, 1883* (Yokohama, 1883), p. 130, and *Proceedings... Tokyo, 1900* (Tokyo, 1901), p. 258.
38. H. Peeke, Nagasaki, to W. Chamberlain, New York, August, 1913, South Japan Mission File, 1913. RCA Archives.

written... I belong to the Lord and desire to work for Him in the way and place He chooses, and should I be convinced that the place is Shimonoseki, I would not dare do other than go. But so far I do not feel it would be best for the work or for myself.[39]

The men of the mission were surprised. They were not used to the women who were their partners in the work asserting themselves, saying what would be best for the work or themselves, or daring to suggest what the will of God might be. The subordinate role of female missionaries was mandated in the institutional structure of the mission. Decisions as to when, where, and how they would their work were not in their own hands. *The Manual... for the use of Candidates...* published by the Board of Foreign Missions in 1885 and used, apparently without revision, well into the 1920s, explicitly delineates the differences between a male missionary and a female missionary. First of all the name "missionary" was not for the women: "Regularly ordained ministers of the Gospel are called *Missionaries*: [...] and all ladies, whether married or single, *Assistant Missionaries*."[40] Decisions as to how the missions were run and how the work would be divided were made in the field in a democratic process in which each missionary had a vote — and each assistant did not.[41]

There were further inequities: single male missionaries in Japan received 100 dollars per annum more, at least, than single women; married women of course received no pay of their own. Furthermore, single women were required to sign a pledge that they would return the costs of the travel and expenses paid by the board if they got married within five years.[42] These inequities and subordinations were mirrors of the larger society which had sent them into the mission field. Yet the education women had been receiving in the high schools, normal schools, colleges, and Bible institutes had given them the self-confidence and the skills to undermine, on occasion, the male dominance of the mission, even while they seemed compliant.

Sara Couch stayed in Nagasaki.

With the partnership of Tomegawa Jun, her former pupil, who was now in her own right a powerful force in the Japanese Protestant community of

39. Sara M. Couch, Nagasaki, to the WBFM, New York, January 11, 1913, South Japan Mission Files (1913), RCA Archives.
40. BFM of the RCA, *Manual ... for Candidates*, p. 3.
41. Ibid., p. 15.
42. Ibid., p. 9, p. 7.

the city, Sara Couch embarked on a new phase in her missionary life, working not through the institution of the girls' school, but in a self-generated round of Bible meetings, Sunday schools, prayer groups, home visits, and the publication of a newspaper especially geared towards young Christian Japanese, *Ochibo*, (i.e. "Gleanings"—a name obviously inspired by the *Mission Gleaner* of the RCA Women's Board of Foreign Missions.) This work would continue to her retirement and beyond.

This study has described not only the formal training that Sara Couch undertook as preparation for mission, but also the informal education she gained "in the field" as her training and expectations clashed with the reality of service as a woman at a foreign mission station. Such "on the job" training took place as the female missionaries negotiated the complex set of relationships they encountered.

Sara Couch was not only a teacher of young Japanese girls; she also worked for a number of years as the subordinate of a Japanese male principal. As a female missionary she had to form good working relationships with her brother missionaries from the West, who in general made the decisions that affected the scope and nature of her work, and also with their wives. She had both living and working relationships not only with other Western female missionaries, but also with Japanese "Bible women" and other workers. She was professionally accountable to both the synod's Board of Foreign Missions and the women's board, representing countless churches and local organizations who supported her financially and emotionally. In addition, she had another set of relationships with the pastor and members of the *Nagasaki Kyokai*, the church called by the missionaries "the Oura church," a small congregation started by the mission but now independent, allied with the Church of Christ in Japan (Nippon *Kirisuto Kyokai*). Finally, she had a long-lasting domestic and professional relationship with Tomegawa Jun, the student who who became first her "Bible helper," then a matron in the Sturges' Seminary, then an equal and sometimes leading partner in the evangelical work in Nagasaki.

Tomegawa Jun matured into a more powerful evangelist than Sara Couch, engaging in preaching tours in Korea, Formosa, and Manchuria, organizing for the Women's Christian Temperance Union (WCTU) and Young Women's Christian Association (YWCA) in Nagasaki, taking the leadership in the publication of *Ochibo*, and being ordained as an elder in the Oura church in 1929, well before women in the RCA were officially approved to hold such leadership positions in the church.[43] Tomegawa San and Miss Couch made a home together: "They lived in the same house, had their table together, and worked as two hearts with but a single thought for many years," as Albertus Pieters put it.[44] Sara Couch's informal "on the job" training as a missionary took place in the nexus of this relationship with all the other relationships she maintained.

One of the primary relationships that contributed to the informal learning process of female missionaries was their collaboration with their male partners in the mission, and their subordination to the male-dominated mission structure. Early leaders of the mission movement had doubted that women could play a powerful role as missionaries and had counseled against sending single females to mission fields. Later, however, this initial hesitation on the part of male missionaries to accept single women as workers alongside them evaporated almost completely, as the usefulness of the women's work became evident — especially in outreach to women and children— and as the women began to outnumber the men. Female and male missionaries were beginning to see themselves as complementary forces in a partnership of service to Christ. One Reformed church pastor described this ideal partnership in 1877, as follows:

> She needs his aggressive energy; he needs her acute, but gentler and more patient spirit. Together, they form that co-partnership of labor, by which, through assisting grace, the whole world shall yet be made to rejoice in the advent of the long desired day.[45]

In reality, the "co-partnership" which men and women able to construct in the mission field was, as this paper has shown in part, far from a partnership of equals.

43. Information on Tomegawa Jun and other Japanese women who were partners and helpers of the RCA women missionaries must be gleaned from the mission records. Published accounts of their work in denominational publications usually omit their full names. For Tomegawa's election as elder of the Oura Church in 1929, see WBFM *Annual Report* 56 (1930), p. 38. Other information is contained in letters of Sara Couch printed in the *Mission Gleaner*, and in annual reports of the WBFM and BFM. The work of Dr. Lane Earns has been invaluable in filling some of these gaps.
44. Albertus Pieters, "In Memoriam," p. 9.
45. Elbert S. Porter, "Women as Missionaries," in *A Manual of the Missions of the Reformed (Dutch) Church in America*, ed. Margaret E. Sangster (New York, 1877), p. 322.

Missionary women — including those of the RCA — are justly celebrated as pioneers who transcended the restrictive role expectations of their times and opened up the possibilities of women's leadership in human affairs, in the approach to God, and in the spread of the Christian gospel. Yet, as Sara Couch's story has revealed, however much missionary women may have been praised and admired, they were not granted authority or autonomy by most male missionaries but had to wrest it from them actively. In 1887, the men gathered for the meeting of the Particular Synod of Albany, no doubt moved by the reports of the missionary fervor of D. L. Moody's Northfield revivals, exclaimed, "We rejoice that Christ still calls men and women to preach to the heathen." But almost a century would pass before the Reformed Church in America would officially recognize women's call to the preaching ministry as legitimate on home territory.[46] The education women received in both secular and church-related institutions actually prepared them for their subordinate roles in the mission field, as long as it emphasized the middle term of the phrase "a scholar, a *lady*, and a Christian." As the century drew to an end, a new focus on professional training and intellectual achievement raised women's discomfort with their roles and helped them forge new identities for themselves as women engaged in the leadership of a practical ministry of compassion.

The women missionaries themselves knew the subversive power of education. A revealing passage printed in the *Mission Gleaner* in the same autumn that Sara Couch first arrived in Japan affirmed the power of education to disrupt cultural and traditional structures oppressing women. The Japanese woman, "needs raising from the position she at present holds, and the means of raising her lies, we believe, in the education Japanese girls are now receiving in Mission schools." The anonymous writer then went even further, saying, "the education will make her rebellious," but that it will strike a "death blow" to oppressive customs "if that rebellion is directed against the degradation of her sex."[47]

The particular customs referred to here were the Japanese *geisha* and *joro* divisions of official prostitution, and their elaborate rituals; these were almost the only professions open to unmarried Japanese women at the turn of the century. The American missionaries — women and men— abhorred

46. Particular Synod of Albany, *Minutes*, 1887, p. 4.
47. "The Education Being Received in Mission Schools," the *Mission Gleaner* 9:6 (September-October, 1892): 11-12.

the practice. They saw their work in the girls' schools as striking a blow at the oppression of Japanese womanhood. At the same time, their own education was tending to make the American women a little more "rebellious" and unwilling to put up with subordination or "degradation" themselves. By teaching the Japanese students to question their culture, they taught themselves to question their own. Sara Couch, at least, in her adoption of Japanese dress, habit, home, and family, and in the stubborn independence of her work with Tomegawa Jun in the city of Nagasaki from 1913 to 1942, seems to have questioned in her own way the shape of the American missionary endeavor in Japan.

Sara Maria Couch was not a typical missionary, it must be said. Few indeed shared the depth or length of her loving adoption of the people among whom she lived. But in some ways, and especially in her early education and training — or lack of it — her story does illumine that of many women who at the end of the nineteenth century found that missionary service overseas was an enormously challenging and satisfying outlet for their new found education and their adventurous spirits. Their churches at home, alas, did not quite know what to do with such spirited and educated females. Couch's story also points up the defects in missionary education of the period. Much energy was spent in drumming up enthusiastic converts: far less time and effort was expended in actually preparing them for their work. Bible institutes such as Moody's valiantly attempted to fill this gap, but the female evangelists they prepared had difficulties adjusting to the different assumptions and practices of the denominational missions. This explains in part the growth of nondenominational and faith missions at this time.[48] Even at the mission-oriented Bible institutes, there was no education that prepared women (or men) for cross-cultural work. Women and men alike arrived in Japan with only the barest knowledge of Japanese culture, history, and traditions, and what they knew had been gained from their own missionary publications, often deeply imbued with the assumption of Western cultural superiority. The great part of missionary education took place "on the job": learning the language at the same time as fulfilling all the duties expected of a boarding school teacher must have been a daunting task. That Sara Couch was able to transcend the limitations of her education and training to achieve her extraordinarily faithful and long service must in

48. For women in independent and faith missions see Dana Robert, *American Women in Mission*.

the end be what she herself would have wished—a witness to the power of the Holy Spirit.

Further studies of the work of Sara Couch and the other women missionaries in Japan must be made. There are more questions to be asked. What was the content of the American women's teaching of the Japanese children? Did they in fact share an education that was in some sense critical of traditional assumptions about women, or did the missionaries try to make the Japanese girls into Western "ladies" who would not be able to rebel against their degradation as women? Did the women like Sara Couch who began to identify strongly with Japanese culture become uncritical of Japanese imperialism towards China, Korea, Russia, and eventually the United States? A hard knot was formed by the intertwining of two cultures that were each in their own way imperialistic, expansionist, patriarchal, materialist, and deeply spiritual — the unpicking of the knot in the lives of Japanese and American Christian women presents many challenges to the historian. The education of Miss Sara Couch continues.

X
The Reformed Church in America and the Ordination of Women:
Personal Memories

Joyce Borgman de Velder

In June, 1979, the General Synod of the Reformed Church in America voted to approve the ordination of women as ministers of the Word. This historic decision came after more than two decades of debate that had been opened by the General Synod in 1955. I was one of the three women whose cases were before the General Synod in 1979, and so this account of that time is personal as well as ecclesiastical.

My own story began in 1950, the year I was born. I was baptized in the First Reformed Church of Fremont, Michigan. My great-grandparents were from Friesland in the Netherlands and Bentheim in northwest Germany. They had come to America largely for religious reasons. My father's family was Christian Reformed. He married into the RCA, but the previous connections remained. I attended the Christian Reformed parochial school from ages five to fifteen. I grew up in a loving, hard-working family. My father was an orchardist. My mother worked at home and managed the orchard's bookkeeping and payroll. Our family was active in the church. In our home, prayer and Bible reading were a sacred part of everyday life.

While a high school student, I had my first experience in ministry serving as a Sunday school teacher in a rural outreach mission of our church. I didn't know it then, but when I look back, I see the beginnings of a call to ministry.

I attended Hope College from 1968-1972. I chose to major in religion, but I had no idea of what I would do with it after graduation. Professor Sang Lee suggested that I go to seminary. I said in response, "women can't go there!" "Sure they can," he said. "Maybe you can teach theology some day!" Next thing I knew I was applying for acceptance into the Master of Divinity Program at Western Theological Seminary. I assured my questioning home church and the Classis of Muskegon, under whose care I came, that I had no intentions of someday being ordained. At the time, I didn't. I had little clarity about what I was going to do.

There were changes in the air, however. I soon learned that in the larger church, papers were being written, debates were starting, and prayers were being prayed for direction about the role of women in ministry. I also learned that some women had gone to seminary—notably Elsie Law who received the M.Div. from Western in 1963, and Charlotte Assink Huitink who received the M. Div. from Western in 1971. By 1972, the same year I enrolled at Western as a Master of Divinity student, the RCA had taken action which permitted the ordination of women to the offices of elder and deacon. This was a significant step for the inclusion of women in ministry for a church that had been wrestling with ordaining women as elders and deacons since 1918. However, it had not made a difference in my home church, which did not, and still does not, ordain women as elders and deacons.

I spent the next four years in seminary — two years at Western, one part-time year at New Brunswick when my husband David and I lived at the Warwick Center in Warwick, New York, and a final year at Western, from which I graduated. My seminary years throughout were a mixture of affirmations and reprovals — a reflection, perhaps, of the continuing struggle in the larger church. For it would be several more years before the church would approve the ordination of women as ministers of the Word. At the outset, it was clearly pointed out to me by the dean of Western Seminary that I was welcome to study in the M. Div. program but that I should not expect to be ordained as a pastor when I finished. During the first year and a half at Western, there were no other women students enrolled in the M.Div. program. I cannot tell you how glad I was to meet Nancy Van

Wyk Philipps when she arrived part way through the second year. There were then two of us. That year, 1973, was the same year in which the first woman in Reformed church history was ordained to the office of the minister of the Word, Joyce Stedge, by the Classis of Rockland-Westchester. Despite the controversy which surrounded her ordination, she stood out for me (even though I did not know her personally at that time) as a living representation of hope and encouragement. Sometime in that second year of seminary, the direction in which I believed God was leading me became much clearer.

In May of 1976, following graduation, I was granted licensure for ordination by the Classis of Muskegon. Late in the fall, David and I left Michigan and arrived in Delmar, New York. The Delmar Reformed Church had hired me to serve as an "Associate in Ministry," a special title devised for one who was not ordained and therefore not eligible for a "call." I was grateful to have the opportunity of ministry and the support of an understanding congregation and pastor, the Rev. Gerard Van Heest.

At this time it seemed as though the denomination was stymied in its efforts to move toward the approval of ordaining women as ministers of the Word. Back in 1958 the General Synod had adopted a recommendation from the Theological Commission which stated: "Scripture nowhere excludes women from eligibility to the offices but always emphasizes their inclusion, prominence, and equal status with men in the Church of Jesus Christ."[1] Though this became the official position of the RCA, tradition continued to be a determining factor in deciding the issue of ordaining women as ministers of the Word. The central problem had to do with the interpretation of the word "persons" in the *Book of Church Order*. Considering the intention of the writers, did the word "persons" include women as well as men? An amendment to substitute the phrase "men and women" for the word "persons" had been defeated by the classes when it was first presented in 1969 by the Classis of Mid-Hudson. Attempts were again made in 1976 and 1977 to have the classes approve the amendment, but each time, there was a failure to obtain the two-thirds vote necessary to amend the *Book of Church Order*.

Other women ministers like myself, as well as many people throughout the denomination, were feeling the frustration of the impasse and asking

1. *Acts and Proceedings of the General Synod* 1958, pp. 328, 331.

how long it would take for the needed change to come. By 1978, more than fifty women had received theological training in seminaries and were already involved in ministry. One of the obvious ironies at this time was that women elders who were so designated were allowed to baptize and administer the Lord's Supper, while the church was unwilling to allow theologically trained women to administer the sacraments. Thus it was that in a special gathering of women in ministry at Stony Point, New York, in April, 1978, the decision was prayerfully made that the time had come to try a new approach. Several of us who had passed the classical examinations for licensure and ordination, and were already serving in churches resolved to go to our respective classes and request ordination. We who had acted upon our callings to ministry, believed that the word "persons" in the *Book of Church Order* included us!

With a mixture of heartfelt conviction and anxiety I made my request known to the Vocational Development Committee of the Classis of Albany, chaired by the Rev. Jim DeVries, who was serving as pastor of the New Baltimore Reformed Church. The committee agreed to recommend that the Classis of Albany grant my request for ordination to the office of Minister of the Word. On June 20, 1978, the Classis of Albany approved that recommendation.

But there was to be a delay. In fact no date was set at this meeting for the ordination. There was understandable concern among some classis delegates as to whether the action of classis was a "proper" thing to do since the denomination had not approved the ordination of women to Ministry of the Word. Subsequent to the meeting the First Reformed Church of Wynantskill, whose pastor was the Rev. David Cooper, filed a complaint against the action of the classis. The complaint was not against ordaining women, but against ordaining women when the General Synod had not yet made an official ruling on the interpretation of the word "persons" in the *Book of Church Order*. This complaint was received by the Permanent Committee on Judicial Business of the Particular Synod of Albany, which had the task of deciding whether to uphold or to dismiss it. Meanwhile, at the fall meeting of Albany Classis on October 17, the Vocational Development Committee was instructed to meet again to discuss the setting of a date for the ordination. The committee met December 21 and recommended that the classis approve the date of March 4, 1979, for the service of ordination. This recommendation was approved at the January 16 meeting of the classis, pending a favorable decision by the Synod of Albany on the report of its Permanent Committee on Judicial Business. But the response was not favorable; on February 17 at a special session of the Particular Synod of Albany, held at the Community Church of Colonie, the committee reported that it

> voted three to one in favor of sustaining the complaint submitted by the First Reformed Church, Wynantskill, New York. Therefore, the Committee recommends for adoption by the Particular Synod of Albany the following resolution: Resolved that the Particular Synod of Albany sustain the complaint of the First Reformed Church, Wynantskill, New York, against the action of Albany Classis in voting to ordain Joyce Borgman de Velder as minister of the Word.[2]

By a vote of 20-12, the Particular Synod of Albany voted to adopt the recommendation of the Judicial Business Committee. A separate motion was approved to direct the Classis of Albany not to ordain J. de Velder as it had voted to do on June 20, 1978.

The ball was now back in the court of the classis. Should the Classis of Albany confirm or complain the decision of the particular synod? At a special session held March 6, the classis decided to complain the action of the Particular Synod of Albany. Over the next several weeks, the Overtures and Judicial Committee of the classis, chaired by the Rev. Allan Janssen of Bethlehem Reformed Church, Selkirk, prepared a complaint which the classis approved on March 20, 1979. Dr. Norman Thomas of New Brunswick Theological Seminary was asked to help. The complaint was then sent to the Judicial Business Committee of the General Synod, which would make its report two months later when the 173rd General Synod convened in June.[3]

Looking back on these ten months of judicatory actions and counteractions, I believe more firmly than ever that the Spirit of God was helping turn the wheels of change that were moving the church. There were times when I felt frustrated with how slowly the wheels were turning; I remember asking myself more than once if my calling to be a minister of the Word was more important than my love and loyalty to the Reformed Church in America, and

2. Minutes of the Particular Synod of Albany (Albany, 1979), p. 78.
3. Allan Janssen has recently discussed these events in his *Gathered at Albany* (Grand Rapids, 1995), pp. 136-46.

whether I should go somewhere else where women were being ordained by the church. There were some who questioned my intentions, thinking that I wanted to be a "test case" and that the timing of my request for ordination was inappropriate, since the General Synod had not ruled on the interpretation of the *Book of Church Order*. One such elder in the Classis of Albany wrote: "The Joyce de Velders, by a variety of pleas and ploys, have persuaded other ministers to support their view that an illegal ordination is better than no ordination at all." During this time, however, I did not have second thoughts about having asked the classis for ordination. I was fully aware that my request for ordination sought action that was contrary to the church's tradition, but I believed in my heart that it was not contrary to the Word of God — nor to the *Book of Church Order*, which, in my reading, permitted the ordinations of persons (including women) who were called by God to ministry and met the requirements for licensure and ordination.

At the time, the ten months of judicial proceedings in the classis and synod seemed long and tedious. I would think of Valerie DeMarinus Miller, L'Anni Hill-Alto, Connie Longhurst, and Klaire Miller, who had already been ordained by their classes in the latter half of 1978 and were hoping now for confirmation by the 1979 General Synod, and then look at my own situation and ask, "Is it worth all this?" But the answer was always, "Yes, if it helps the church to be decisive about ordaining women and opens the way for other qualified women to seek ordination." While I often felt emotionally stressed during those months, I did not give up faith in God or in the cause. Prayer and the support of my family and the faith community held me up. Even though there were differences of opinion within the classis regarding how best to respond to my request for ordination (including the unrelenting objections of a woman elder delegate in the church I was serving), I was comforted and sustained by the respect, understanding, and personal support given to me by most people, wherever they stood on the issue.

The full importance of the events of those months became obvious only later. In looking back, I know that I did not fully anticipate how my request (and those of my sisters in ministry) would help place the issue of the ordination of women before the General Synod. But it became clear that the judicial process would serve a crucial role in succeeding, where amendments had failed, to bring about a decision in the RCA to open the office of Minister of the Word to women. Thus in June of that year, the 173rd General Synod met in Holland, Michigan, and on Wednesday, June 13, received its Judicial

Business Committee report on the complaint from the Classis of Albany against the action of the particular synod concerning my ordination and on two other complaints by individuals against the particular synods of New York and New Jersey, which had upheld the respecitive ordinations of Valerie DeMarinus Miller and L'Anni Hill-Alto. The committee judged that although the ordination of women represented a change in church custom and practice, nonetheless to ordain women does not violate the understanding or requirements of the *Book of Church Order*; and, following the findings of the committee, the synod voted (150-115) to sustain the complaint of the Classis of Albany against the Particular Synod of Albany in my case and to dismiss the other two complaints.

I was not a delegate to the 173rd General Synod, but I was present the day the vote was taken and sitting in the rows of seats behind the delegates, which were reserved for guests. I sat, so to speak, on the edge of my seat, through the day, listening, wondering, praying, hoping for this decision that would be so definitive for my life and calling, and for that of my sisters in ministry. I had been wondering how I and others would react when the outcome of the vote was announced. If the recommendation was supported, would we be able to contain our joy? If it was defeated, would we have the emotional and spiritual strength of will to keep pressing for this change? When the vote was announced, and the words sank in, I remember feeling a deep sense of relief and gratitude. I turned to those around me and we quietly hugged each other. There was a part of me that wanted to stand up and shout! But the joy I felt was subdued by the memory of eight years of preparation, waiting, and struggle to hear this confirmation, and by the awareness that there were many delegates to the synod for whom this decision was a deep disappointment. Someone asked me shortly afterward how I felt. I remember saying something to the effect that it was a "bittersweet" moment for me: we truly had something to celebrate — something to show for the faithful efforts of the past that had begun even before I was born, something for which to praise God for the way God's Spirit was leading the church. But there were also wounds that were in need of healing, and there were yet "miles to go" before the Reformed Church in America would fully speak with one voice on the ordination of women to ministry.

That same summer of 1979, on Sunday, July 15, I was ordained by the Classis of Albany at the Delmar Reformed Church. It was a celebration of ministry — the ministry of God's Spirit in the church and the shared ministry of God's faithful people, women and men, young and old together. The Rev. Gerard Van Heest, then pastor at Delmar, preached a sermon from Acts 10 entitled, "The Spirit Continues to Teach."

Almost twenty years have passed by since those events. I have now served more than fifteen years as the pastor of the Old Saratoga Reformed Church in Schuylerville, New York. Today there are more than 100 women ordained in the Reformed Church in America, and more to come. Many people through the years have been instrumental, directly or indirectly, in the historic change which the ordination of women brought to the Reformed Church in America. Missionary women, Women's Boards of Foreign Missions, Reformed Church Women, the Commission on Women, other agencies and commissions of the RCA, church leaders, college and seminary professors, classes, and synods have all played a part.

I am humbly grateful to have, with my sisters in ministry and with all who helped bring the church to this day, played a small part in the ordination of women to ministry. It is my faith-filled conviction that God was and is at work in the life of the church. I hope these reflections will be a testimony to those who hear them, that the Spirit of God leads and moves in surprising and unpredictable ways and is ever challenging and strengthening the body of Christ for ministry in the world.

XI

The Decline, Fall, and Rise of Women in the Reformed Church in America, 1947-1997

Carol W. Hageman

This essay will be a retrospective on my many years serving the Reformed church as a lay woman volunteer on the Women's Board of Domestic Missions (WBDM) and its successors the Board of North American Missions and the General Program Council. I will trace some of the activity and acceptance of women in the Reformed church over a period of almost fifty years, and specifically the diminution of the place and influence of lay women in its boards and agencies. It occurs to me that the reader may find disproportionate emphasis on domestic missions here, but that is the setting in which I worked; the essay will necessarily be personal, since my own experience is my main qualification for writing it.

A note about nomenclature: there have been many changes in the last forty years and I will try not to be offensive in the course of this essay, but I hope to be forgiven if I slip into old, but to me familiar, terminology. The blessed word "chairman" is a case in point. Having been brought up to consider the word "man" to be generic for human being, I was just as comfortable being addressed as Madam Chairman as I was addressing someone else as Mr. Chairman—thinking one no more an oxymoron than the other redundant.

The Women's Board of Domestic Missions

I was first approached to serve as a member-at-large of the Women's Board of Domestic Missions in 1947, having been married two years to a clergyman in the Reformed church—a unique position in my family, which was a very devout, active family in the Reformed church without any ministerial history. My home church was very supportive of and interested in mission, but I believe I was really aware only of foreign missionary activity. So this invitation came to a completely uninitiated young woman. I was not alone in my ignorance, however. When I was asked to speak to the Women's Missionary Society of my home church (my mother's society) a little later about my newfound knowledge and interest, the local newspaper described me as Mrs. Howard Hageman, the domestic member of the Board of Missions!

That there were Women's Boards of Missions, both Foreign and Domestic, never caused me any question until much later. I did a little digging into historical papers and that wonderfully revealing little book, *Fifty Years in Foreign Fields*,[1] I discovered that the Woman's Board of Foreign Missions (WBFM) was organized in 1875 by a group of concerned women who had to badger the General Synod into allowing them to address certain specified injustices to women in China—this problem having been brought to their attention by the revered China missionary, David Abeel. In 1882, a brief seven years later, a group of women who described themselves as acting "timidly and prayerfully," responded to a *request* of the General Synod's Board of Domestic Missions to take up missionary work in the homeland! It hadn't taken the General Synod very long to appreciate the ability of women, particularly in the field of fundraising. Little did they know how aggressive and successful these women would be in initiating and administering new work.

Be that as it may, I soon found myself immersed in the home mission work. The board was comprised of an executive committee and members at large. The members at large were a fairly goodly number, representing various

---

1. Mary E. A. Chamberlain, *Fifty Years in Foreign Fields. China, Japan, Inda, Arabia. A History of Five Decades of the Woman's Board of Foreign Missions, Reformed Church in America* (New York, 1925).

areas of the church. The executive committee met monthly and all members at large were invited and received minutes of all meetings. However, the women's board was not about to use any more money on itself than was absolutely necessary, so there was no budget item for board travel. That precluded many who lived at a distance from attending, since all the executive committee meetings were held in New York City. However, the membership generally wanted it that way, in order that as much money as possible could go directly into field work. Distance did not seem to diminish interest and commitment. I remember well women coming to New York City by train from the Midwest, sitting up, traveling coach all the way and sharing with us the bag lunches we brought for the meeting day! I have a funny, sweet memory of a dear old lady from the West who had a real concern that Howard and I (so young at the time) were living and working in the city of Newark. For, she said, when she came into New York City she could smell the evil in the air! I think it was the smoke from the coal-powered locomotives trapped in the tunnels of Grand Central Station—but I was and still am touched by her innocent concern. At any rate, I soon became a member of the executive committee, probably because of proximity.

I must mention the names of some of the women who led the board in the late '40s when I entered the scene. Mary Brinig, on staff of Marble Collegiate Church in New York, was president, having just succeeded Ruth Peale. Helen Brickman was our executive; Blanch Cleaver, also from Marble, was treasurer; Francis Brink, secretary; Lillian Pool chaired the Indian American committee to which I was assigned; and Catherine Hoffman chaired the Kentucky Committee. (You might notice that we were not given to fancy committee names; what you heard was what you got.) There were represented a large number of honorable names in the Reformed church as well—Van Brunt, Scudder, Bayles, Voslousky, Cobb, Vruwink, Soeter, Demarest, Joldersma—to mention just a few.

Our concerns were many. In addition to its fields of missionary work—the Indian-American fields and Kentucky—the board also ministered to new Americans (foreign-language work in the cities), subsidized parsonages for churches aided by the synod's board, and granted scholarships to young people. It also assisted the Department of Youth, directed by Marion Van Horne. And there was more. At my first board meeting, as I remember, after we had heard the reports of all these fields, including reports of work among Italian-Americans in Newburg, New York, and Newark, New Jersey, a new concern was voiced about the Alaskan Indians on Japanski Island, and another report was presented on the work of the John Milton Society for the blind, and after that there was a considerable discussion to be sure that our fundraising not conflict with the General Synod's new Advance Fund appeal.

There was some cooperation with General Synod's Board of Domestic Missions. The synod's board proved not to be interested in a proposed joint work among the Alaskan Indians, but it did increasingly ask the women to subsidize parsonages for supported churches and also to give monies for small needs in these churches. The women were also invited to join synod's board in certain city works—a natural extension of their established foreign-language work.

Some things never change—or at least come around again and again. In the late 1940s there was discussion of moving the WBDM office to the Midwest. It was decided instead to increase the at-large membership and even to put $800 in the budget for necessary travel.

A word about committee work. The board's committees carried a great deal of administrative responsibility, for the entire work of the WBDM was supervised by one executive secretary and a small clerical and bookkeeping staff. For my part, I was assigned to the Indian-American Committee and embarked on another learning experience. Lillian Pool chaired the committee and obviously had for some time, for her knowledge of and concerned care for the fields, the missionaries and the people of our Indian churches was extensive, very deep and real. It speaks volumes, I think, of the women's administration of these fields that not only were ordained missionaries employed by the board but also that their relationships with the committees were warm and trusting. Each chairwoman knew her field intimately and was concerned for those *converted* to Christianity. In addition to the nuts and bolts of maintaining buildings and the support material, the lives of many of our Indian Christians were a real item for prayer and support. A concern to make higher education available for some of those Indian Christians occupied much time, effort, and prayer at our meetings. One of the board's projects was the financial and personnel support of the Cook Christian Training School for Indian Americans, and during my tenure on the board several of our students went on to Reformed church colleges. For all the attendant problems, the ultimate successes of these students as they returned to leadership positions in their tribal life were greeted with joy.

While reading through some of the old minutes, I came across a small but interesting change. In 1949, for the first time, we were identified by our given names with our husbands' in parentheses.

Merger with the Synod's Board

I must set the stage now for the coming mergers of boards and agencies. You can read lofty reasons for integrating work, and later for preparing for ecumenical work, by structuring ourselves to work more easily with larger denominations and councils. But my own opinion is that *money*—the acquisition and use thereof—had an awful lot to do with it. At one point, all four boards of mission, and to a lesser degree, the Board of Education, were competing in the church for the same dollar. This competition really did not change even after the consolidation of the boards; the tug of war would just move into board debate and budget, and so become a little less public. (Now, as I understand it, we are moving back to something like square one again.) However, the four boards' competition did make the local churches *very* much aware of the many works of their national church. We all had speakers' bureaus (many times comprised of board members) all ready and willing, even anxious, to address any society or church meeting needing a program. Some, particularly missionaries, were spectacularly successful at touching both the heart-strings and the purse-strings. It was a bit of a touchy situation, and, being in something of an underdog position, the WBDM was very careful to work within the guidelines determined by General Synod.

It was in 1949 that the board voted to approve the concept of union with the synod's Board of Domestic Missions. An appropriate planning committee was named by both boards, with Helen Brickman (our executive) and Richard Vanden Berg (her counterpart) acting as consultants. Since General Synod had already approved the merger we really didn't have much wiggle room. A study was also underway for a combined foreign and domestic women's work in the event (or rather when) the domestic boards merged. The foreign boards had already merged.

As union of the boards progressed, the WBDM embarked with synod's board in support of the East Harlem Protestant Parish, a new and forward-looking ecumenical work addressing "the tremendous new home missionary needs."

The committee for board union worked hard and long on the plan. It even dared to think the unthinkable—the appointment of *two* executive secretaries. All board members were contacted to determine their availability for service on the new board, nominating lists were prepared, and articles were written for the *Church Herald* trying to explain to the church, and particularly to the women who had given so much time to the two women's boards, that there would be a place for them in the membership of the new Department of Women's Work. It was not easy to explain that to women who had carried so much responsibility in the past. You did not need to be a genius to understand that the new Department of Women's Work would be seen as a fundraising arm of the administrative boards, without voice, so to speak.

The two full boards of domestic missions met together at Buck Hill Falls in April, 1950, and acted on the refinements of the merger. In May, the minutes of the WBDM reveal a very touching last meeting, remembering the many years the board had been in operation and its long list of accomplishments, the literally hundreds of women devoted to the cause, our devoted and accomplished missionaries, the legacies left to continue the work, the replacing of old sod houses on the "frontier," Christmas boxes, scholarships for training students and youths, the lives, the printed and spoken words used by the Reformed church to win the United States for Christ, and last, but certainly not least, the dollars lovingly given—from a total of $2,532 reported after the first year and a half of the board's existence, to its sixty-seventh year, reporting over $231,000. I quote: "Thanks to God for each member who responded with heart as well as ears" and a "rededication each day of our lives and our efforts." A special program and tribute to former members and missionaries was presented at the end of the meeting, which closed with a poem written by Cornelia Bedell: "Time marches on— We Fear Not." How quickly things change. It all sounds so innocent and quaint today.[2]

There was much to be learned as the new Board of Domestic Missions faced the future. To begin with, there was the matter of the gender of the membership. It was finally decided that representation from each former board would be prorated on the amount of money each brought to the merger. Hence there would be forty-eight members, twenty-seven men and twenty-one women: our first step downhill. I have a couple of vivid memories of the early meetings. We traveled to meetings scheduled in

2. Minutes of the Women's Board of Domestic Missions, May 9, 1950, p. 2, and attached document entitled, "What is the WBDM?"

various churches in the denomination. In doing so, we learned to spend money! No longer suffering coach travel, we women were introduced to the glories of the Pullman car. There were many hilarious moments as we discovered the mysteries of roomettes and just what you had to look under to find the convenience you needed. Those little units were gems of engineering. Pity the long-suffering Pullman porter—for as I remember, in some mysterious way, we women found ourselves in one car while our male counterparts were safely elsewhere.

Another incident is burned into my memory. One evening on the train, a very courtly old-school gentleman member escorted me through several sliding doors between cars as we progressed to the dining car (no more sack lunches). The soul of courtesy, he helped me through the menu and then we discussed the organizational problems facing us. When we reached the touchy subject of executive staff, he, in all earnestness, carefully asked me if I really thought the denomination would take a woman executive seriously? At that moment, it would have been easy to return to sitting up in the coach with my independence intact. However, we were off and running and gradually there developed a mutually uneasy trust. We settled for two and then three executives—two men and one woman, of course.

The 1950s began. The new board continued the work the two boards had done in the past. The synod's board had administered—besides church extension and salary supplement—the work at Brewton and Mexico. It took an uprising of the Indians in Chiapas early this year to remind some of our churches that the Reformed church has had work there together with the Presbyterians for many, many years. Some of the hardships and injustices we hear about today are the very same I remember from early exposure to that mission. I can't help but wonder what is happening to all the wonderful Indian folk who embraced their place in Christ's church at great cost to themselves, who would walk miles in that primitive land to spend whole days in worship.

There was also much new activity in Canada with the arrival of many folk from the Netherlands. We couldn't let the Christian Reformed church have them all, neither could we work with that church, so we each established an arm of our stateside churches in Canada. Cooperation with the Presbyterian or United Churches of Canada was considered, but seemingly could not work. Also on our side of the border there was an increased emphasis on urban work and there came a new ministry among the Jews in Passaic County, New Jersey.

While we traveled in relative comfort to our meetings, we did save money by visiting congregations across the country and staying with church members, except when we met in New York City where it was deemed inadvisable. Our visitations put a great strain on the congregations, for they fed and housed us and put up with meetings that lasted often well into the night. However, I learned a lot during this time too—for instance, how a dairy farm works, and that corn cribs (if that is the right term) look alarmingly like oil storage tanks. And I know that I stayed with many wonderful families and forged strong ties of mutual respect as well as concern for people living in need in our country of privilege.

I learned other, more difficult things as we ventured out of New York City for our meetings. I came to realize that I was among the seeming few who were not related to, or educated with, half of the Reformed church! It seems that I had led a rather sheltered life, and at a very deep level I was shocked to discover that the Christianity of my section of the church—and hence my own—was viewed by many as being somewhat less than it ought to be, or even suspect. That was hard. To this day I do not know why I did not "pack it in" and return to the safety of my church in Newark where I was accepted without question. I am ever grateful that I did not, for it made me consider my faith more seriously, and, I hope, mature in it. However, if there are any among my readers who sometimes feel that in the Reformed church they have landed on some alien planet, take heart; you will survive and be the better for it!

By the middle of the '50s the board was functioning very well and although we had many heated debates, a good spirit prevailed and with the work went a lot of fun. And *much* good work was accomplished. In September of 1957, we entered into a contract to participate in the Interchurch Center, with a $5,000 capital contribution and a $45,000 second mortgage. Also in this period we entered a joint venture with the other boards to be known as Children's Work. Foreign language was dropped from my committee's name and we became plain "Inner City." You notice that our committees still carried pretty plain-Jane names.

I will ask your pardon again as I make another value judgment. After all the dust had settled, the board's pattern of work seemed to follow in this order of importance: church extension (building fund) and salary supplement, Canada, Mexico, Brewton, City, Kentucky, Indian American, evangelism and women's work. I believe the amount of ink devoted to each item in the board minutes would bear me out. As the influence of the lay women diminished, so did the interest in their concerns. Again it was the money, of course. I can remember debates over budget allocations when, alas, the cry of the brothers depending on salary supplement was clearly heard, but the cry of the Indian American brother could not be heard so clearly.

During the late 1950s, the last years of my membership on the board, many changes were taking place. A dramatic change was the growing independence of our mission churches on the fields, as well as the churches in Canada. Our executive staff enlarged to three, with the support of "field secretaries" or representatives, classical agents, all of whom had to do with church extension, and an enlarged office staff to match. And foreshadowing mergers yet to come, there developed a controversy over board names. The foreign board had adopted the name, "Christian World Missions," which we thought a bit presumptuous. So began a debate about a more appropriate name for "Domestic Missions." Finally, the name "Board of North American Missions" emerged—a name which, I must confess, I always thought unfortunate if only because it is difficult to fit on a check!

Also in that period, I became a member of the Department of Urban Work, Division of Home Missions, National Council of Churches of Christ in America (try getting that on a check) and was authorized, after much badgering by my board, to attend a workshop entitled, "The Effective City Church." Once again I learned a lot. First I discovered I was one of few if any laypeople attending, not employed in the work. (You know how the line goes, "Yes of course, you are the chair of a committee, but what do you *do*?) Second, I seemed to be one of the few actively connected with a city parish outside of New York City. Third, I soon realized that what they meant was the *efficient* rather than the *effective* city church. I was not happy, and for me the experience foreshadowed an unhappy future for volunteer women.

In the fall of 1958, I finally retired from the board.

The General Program Council

Then, somehow, after an appropriate lapse of time I was back—to a very changed world! Serious discussions were under way toward a complete restructuring of our church's boards and agencies. A professional organization knowledgeable in the structure of these corporate mergers, Edward Hay and Associates, had been engaged to assist in the planning. We had come a long way from our relatively innocent merger in 1950 designed by a committee. Of course, this merger was much more complex. A serious decision had been made, I presume by the General Synod, to change totally the character of the boards from administrative to policy-making, with an executive structure shaped like a pyramid and patterned closely after our larger sister denominations, the National Council and, of course, industry. Accountability was the banner under which all this was moving. The newly merged entity was to be called the General Program Council. I grieve over the day when our church decided to trade the word "mission" for "program." Oh, I know that that honorable old word had fallen on evil days and had become the butt of nasty jokes. It also, it must be said, had been used to cover some grave injustices done in the name of the church in the past. However, somehow "program" indicates to me something we control. "Mission," on the other hand, still carries for the me the charge given us by our Lord— controled by him. But that is another essay.

As the merger drew near, the several boards and agencies were to nominate eight people to be elected by the General Synod to the new General Program Council. It is an understatement to say this was not a happy time for women. From the minutes, I find that, to its everlasting credit, the Board of North American Missions nominated four women and four men; the world board, two women and six men; stewardship council, one woman and seven men; and I do not have the record for the boards of education and pensions. The final organization approved by the General Synod in 1968 called for a board of sixty-one, including forty-five from the various classes and fifteen nominated by the General Synod. At that time, all classis members would be male, leaving fifteen slots to be filled, in the best of all worlds, by women. As we became more sensitive to the needs of others within our church, these fifteen places were shared with youth, the Black Council, American Indian Council, and Asian Council. Lay women really hit bottom in our downhill slide!

In the fall of 1968, there was a joint meeting of all the boards and agencies together with the new General Program Council to transfer programs and services formally, recommend a revised budget, and, in the words of the minutes, "terminate" (!) members of the boards and agencies.

I trust you will forgive yet another observation from my perspective and with it a word of caution. It is laudable to try in every way to use the gifts of time, talents, and money that God has given us as efficiently and effectively as possible. However, we must be careful lest in our zeal for efficiency, we become too bureaucratic and suffer the results we see in government all around us, especially the growing apathy of our people. Or to put the warning in other terms: we need to be careful not to become so priestly that our churches become more congregational.

Needless to say, the executive staff of the new board was predominantly male. The first president of the board was Frederick Olert, a Reformed church minister serving, I believe, a Presbyterian church at the time. I served for a time as vice president. Lest you find that reassuring, let me recall for you the esteem that vice presidents generally hold in our federal government. Can you even remember many? We had never heard of the glass ceiling at that time, but it was surely there. That blessed office of vice president seems often to be a token reserved for women. (I held it on the Newark Board of Education, too.) At any rate, after a short term I once again, and finally, retired. I will say no more about the General Program Council; its good work has been well documented by Russell Gasero for its twenty-fifth anniversary.[3]

Rising Again

And there, dear friends, my story apparently ends sadly. Indeed, when I was generously invited to attend the final meeting of the General Program Council in 1993, I was saddened by the small number of lay women at the gala dinner who were not in staff or support positions. Along with the hurt of the decline of lay women on our mission boards, I felt the distinct sense of loss of a hands-on experience. I suppose I was too long in the parish to find satisfaction in a purely "objective" role; I missed, and still miss, knowing the people to whom we minister—a more personal involvement with and appreciation of our brothers and sisters. You can understand why this exercise of immersion in the past came at first to be titled, "The Decline and Fall of Women in the Reformed Church."

But that is not really the end of the story. For there has been a "rising again," and I would like to conclude on a hopeful note by calling attention to it.

After several abortive starts, the Department of Women's Work evolved into that very important organization we know today as Reformed Church

3. Russell Gasero, *Twenty-five Years of the General Program Council.* To appear in the "Occasional Papers of the RCA Historical Society" series, published by the RCA Archives.

Women's Ministries and I would direct your thinking to the important part these lay women play in our church life, particularly at the local level. Although still excluded in large part from the administrative center, they have developed a very strong organization devoted to helping lay women realize their potential within the church. They emphasize strengthening personal and corporate devotional life and have instituted very inventive programs for women to contribute to work on our various fields, both financially and physically. It is not an easy road they have traveled, and that they have not given up in the face of a series of rebuffs is an indication of their devotion to their Lord and his Church. They have persisted in the full knowledge that they have a real place in God's order of things. There is no doubt in my mind that a body of women at prayer can accomplish wonderful things and that power is evidenced in our church today through Reformed Church Women's Ministries.

Meanwhile, the need for women to take their rightful place in the ordained ministry of our church surfaced and was gradually and painfully addressed. First we had ordained female deacons in the local churches—women's natural ministry, some argued. Then came the ordination of women as elders—a little more daring step. Finally, after much debate and hurt, came the ordination of women to the ministry of Word and sacrament, as related in the essay by Joyce DeVelder. It always seemed immoral to me that the church urged young women to study at its seminaries and urged the seminaries to open their doors to them, with classis sponsorship, only to deny ordination upon completion of the work. It also seemed sad to me that so much of the debate appeared to hinge on the legal nicety of whether or not the "persons" referred to in the *Book of Church Order* included women. However, to a large degree that debate is well behind us and at long last the church is beginning to experience the ministry of these remarkable and gifted women. After its long history of denying them their unique presence in Word and sacrament, the church is experiencing the full nature of God as revealed by Christ Jesus. I hope you will not consider me blasphemous if I detect an echo of the recovery of that "stone which the builders rejected (Ps. 118:22)."

I hope that this history has not been too personal, too negative, or too opinionated. If so, you may chalk it up to my advanced years. I do want you to know how privileged I feel to have had an active part in our church life. I am full of gratitude, for I have known the strength, the spirit, and the love that abound in our church and I love it dearly.

XII
New Brunswick Theological Seminary Women Past and Present

Mary Kansfield

In the fall of 1992, our family received an invitation from New Brunswick Seminary's Board of Trustees to visit the seminary in consideration of a call for my husband to become president. That visit included an evening meeting with students at New Brunswick Seminary's New York campus. It was the first evening of the fall semester, and, plastic punch glass in hand, I joined two middle-aged women students who were discussing their fall courses. As one woman confessed to job stress and family demands, she voiced her fear that she could not possibly handle two courses that semester. The course on Barth and Tillich would simply be one course too much.

After patiently listening, the second student became agitated and said in an authoritative tone, "You can manage both courses, and I'm going to tell you how you're going to do it. I'm going to help you. While I never cared much for either Barth or Tillich, I have had that course, and I will help you get through it."

Two things became defined in that pivotal conversation. I heard each woman making a commitment to the process of training for ministerial leadership, and I also heard each woman engaging herself in some form of sacrifice which would be integral to the training process.

My perception of their sacrifice and the sacrifice of other women seminarians led me to conduct a survey of New Brunswick Theological Seminary women seminarians in 1995. In that survey I sought to identify the characteristics which distinguish the women who currently attend New Brunswick Theological Seminary.[1] To provide a context for the characteristics identified in the survey, I examined the historical records of women whose names are found in the earliest history of New Brunswick Theological Seminary. This essay seeks to identify what characteristics distinguish the lives of the women who played a role in New Brunswick Seminary's early history and to determine how these characteristics compare with those of today's women seminarians.

Women in New Brunswick Theological Seminary's Early History

It should come as no surprise to anyone that the early years of the seminary's history, as recorded in the minutes of the General Synod of the Reformed Church in America and the seminary's own histories, is dominated by men. Few references to women can be found.[2] This lack robs us of material that would otherwise have provided for colorful reading. Surely Mrs. Livingston, the wife of the seminary's first professor, had something to say about their dreadful move from New York City to the "outback" of New Brunswick in 1810. Leaving behind an established and privileged life in New York City for an untried and new life in New Brunswick had to entail considerable sacrifice on her part, and for this reason Sarah Livingston must have been an interesting person in her own right.[3]

1. I am grateful to Joan deVelder, who assisted me in putting together the survey form, thereby making the data manageable to tabulate.
2. These histories include: *Centennial of the Theological Seminary of the Reformed Church in America* (New York, 1885); Edward Tanjore Corwin, *A Digest of Synodical Legislation of the Reformed Church in America* (New York, 1906); idem., *A Manual of the Reformed Church in America 1628-1878* (New York, 1869), Charles E. Corwin, *A Manual of the Reformed Church in America 1628-1922* (New York, 1922), pp. 119-140; Howard G. Hageman, *Two Centuries Plus: The Story of New Brunswick Seminary*, (Grand Rapids, 1984); Richard P. McCormick, *Rutgers: A Bicentennial History* (New Brunswick, 1966).
3. See Alexander Gunn, *Memoir of the Rev. John H. Livingston* (New York, 1829), pp. 249-250, 332-333.

But there were women in New Brunswick Seminary's early history. By 1800, many involved church women had joined together in church groups to form "cent societies." Each woman member tried weekly to save a penny out of her household allowance. The money was to be used to provide scholarship aid to needy seminary students.[4] This early form of seminary support necessarily involved the honing of domestic skills and careful household management along with considerable sacrifice on the part of these dedicated women. It should be noted that their contributions were earmarked, from the start, for support of needy seminary students and not for the seminary's general fund.

In the published records of New Brunswick Seminary, the first reference to an individual woman appears in 1815. Miss Rebecca Knox bequeathed $2,000 to the seminary, the interest of which was specifically designated to support indigent students.[5] Little is known about Rebecca Knox, except that she was from Philadelphia, a member of the Crown Street Dutch Reformed Church of which Dr. Jacob Brodhead was pastor, and that she was a single person.[6]

In May, 1828, three years after Dr. Livingston's death, the forerunner of the present day Student Financial Aid office was created. Known first as the Education Society, this voluntary society was composed of individuals interested in the seminary.[7] Its purpose was missionary and student financial support, and its constitutional articles specified that "any donation of $1,500 or more, for the founding of a scholarship, was to be distinguished by the name of the donor."[8] In the lists of these donors, the names of women appear along with the names of male donors. Who were these women? What prompted their giving and at what personal cost?[9]

Among the more than thirty portraits that the seminary owns today, only two are of women. They are of Ann Hertzog and Mary Board. Both women are distinguished by their monetary gifts to New Brunswick Seminary. What we know of their identity, however, is limited.

4. Corwin, *Digest,* 120. See also *Minutes of the General Synod* (hereafter *MGS*) 1818, p. 18; 1820, p. 46.
5. *MGS,* 1815, 43.
6. *Centennial of the Theological Seminary of the Reformed Church in America* (New York, 1885), p. 406.
7. Ibid. The work of the Education Society was later incorporated by the General Synod into the Board of Education.
8. Ibid., p. 407.
9. Ibid., pp. 407-409.

The years following 1840 were years of steady student growth. A new Covenant between Rutgers College and the Seminary, in that year, paved the way for the separation of the two institutions, and by 1855 funding was sought to build a new Theological Hall at an estimated cost of $40,000. Hopes were pinned on a Collegiate Church gift of $25,000, which was the needed minimum amount mandated by the General Synod. These hopes soon changed to disappointment when the Collegiate consistory revealed that no such gift would be forthcoming.[10] It is at this point that a woman from Philadelphia named Ann Hertzog becomes known to us by her offer to fund the new theological hall.

Ann Hertzog and her husband, Peter Hertzog, lived in Philadelphia, where they were involved members of the Crown Street Reformed Dutch Church, and later Third Reformed Dutch Church. Peter, a successful businessman, died in 1842. They had no children. Wishing to honor her husband in some significant way, Ann Hertzog was urged by her confidential friend, the Rev. Dr. John Ludlow, to consider endowing a professorship at the seminary. This she did in her will in the amount of $25,000. However, when it became known to her that a building was needed, Ann Hertzog decided not only to contribute her gift immediately, but also to add $5,000 to the needed amount, thus providing $30,000 to construct The Peter Hertzog Theological Hall. To this amount she added $800 for window shades, and in her will an additional gift of $10,000 was left to the seminary.

What do we know about Ann Hertzog as a person? She is described in the 1866 *Minutes of General Synod* this way:

> Mrs. Anna (sic) Hertzog was a woman of strong mind and well developed character. She was prudent and wise, self-reliant and yet modest, active and self-contained, dignified and somewhat quaint in manner and speech, eminently pious and attached to the Church and the orthodox faith, kind-hearted and benevolent. Down to her last year of life (80 years of age) she transacted her own business, and managed her household affairs with old-fashioned exactness and regularity. She was scrupulously punctual at church, and manifested unfailing interest in every thing that concerned its welfare.[11]

10. Ibid., p. 127.
11. *MGS*, 1866, pp. 111-112. See also E.T. Corwin, *Manual*, pp. 109-110.

Ann Hertzog must have liked to have things done well. What else would prompt her to give $5,000 beyond the necessary $25,000? And money for window shades? It would seem that details were important to Ann Hertzog, and in her will she left $10,000 as a final gift. Obviously a Christian woman of independent means, I marvel at her generosity and her obvious faith that giving during her own lifetime would not jeopardize her retirement savings and future well being. It is impressive that a woman alone in 1855, without her married partner, made such a monumental commitment.

Mary Board was also a major donor to the seminary. Little is known about her. We don't know the years of her life, although we know she was elderly and a widow at the time she was asked by James A. H. Cornell to consider a gift to the seminary. This she did in the amount of $3,000 which was used to purchase books for the library. In addition, Mary Board signed a promissory note for $10,000, and by 1876 $4,200 had been paid on the promissory note. The Board of Superintendents used this income to reduce the seminary's debt. Additionally, the Board of Superintendents authorized and paid out $2,426 for repairs to Hertzog Hall based on the anticipated realization of the promised income which remained from the promissory note. At this point we learn of tragedy. Mary Board, whose promissory note depended on the sale of her farm land, fell victim to economic recession and was unable to sell the land to pay off the promissory note. Not only was she unable to fulfill her promissory note, but the entire matter required a vote of the General Synod to excuse her from her obligation.[12] How upsetting and embarrassing this must have been for Mary Board. She had dared to be brave. She trusted the future to God's providence and placed herself at financial risk on behalf of training future leaders in Christ's church and the Reformed church in particular. When giving places us at personal risk, it is indeed sacrificial.

One last observation about Rebecca Knox, Ann Hertzog, and Mary Board. All three of these donors were women who were unmarried or whose husbands had died prior to the time of their commitment to the seminary. They all had counsel from their families, their friends, and their pastors. The decision to make financial commitments to the seminary, however, ultimately was made by each woman alone. To do so required from each of these women tremendous strength, willingness to risk making a commitment, and faith that what each was doing as God's servant would make a difference.

12. *MGS*, 1876, pp. 406, 439, 441.

New Brunswick Theological Seminary Women Today

If the commitment of women in the early history of the seminary, especially that of Rebecca Knox, Ann Hertzog, and Mary Board, required various forms of personal sacrifice, what can be said about the identity of women seminarians today? At what points do their commitments to attend seminary emulate the personal sacrifices of these women from New Brunswick Seminary's early history?

In part, this question is answered by data collected from a survey of women attending New Brunswick Theological Seminary. Their collective profile follows.[13]

The context from which women seminarians come today is broad and varied. While a few women enter seminary shortly following their graduation from college or come to the seminary in their retirement years, most are in their mid-forties.[14] Their academic credentials predominantly reflect completion of bachelor's level work, although advanced degrees are often present. A very small number of women have no college-level degree.[15]

13. Responses to these questions are based on a survey of NBTS women seminarians undertaken by the author in 1995. Of 101 women registered, survey forms were given to 99 women seminarians. Forty-two completed forms were returned by 11 women from the New York campus and by 31 women from the New Brunswick campus making a 42 percent rate of return.

   According to ATS data from the 1994-95 academic year, the total student body of men and women enrolled in the fall of 1994 numbered 211. Of these 211 students, 43 were enrolled at the New York campus, and 168 were enrolled at the New Brunswick campus. Full time students numbered 41, and part-time students totaled 170. Overall, the racial composition of the student body was 49% White, 37% Black, 8% Asian and 2% Hispanic. Eighty-five percent of the student body were members of 8 oldline denominations. Altogether more than 30 different religious traditions were represented in the student body. The gender composition of the seminary was 101 or 48% women. Reformed Church in America students totaled 57 of whom 33 were men and 24 were women. (In 1871, the all time high enrollment for RCA students, that number also stood at 57, although all were white males at that time.)

14. The women ranged in age from 27 to 65 years, with 46.54 the average age and 47 the median age. At the time they began taking classes, the youngest student was 24 and the oldest was 61, with the average age being 41.3 years and the median age 41 years.

15. When these women began seminary, 29 of the women had bachelor level degrees, 7 held masters degrees, 2 held doctoral degrees, 1 had an R.N. degree, and 3 women had no degree.

Most women currently at New Brunswick Theological Seminary attend on a part-time basis.[16] Almost all commute to the seminary by car or train. On average, the drive by car involves 48 miles of round trip travel, with virtually no way to escape high density urban traffic patterns.

The majority of women in seminary today arrive intending to complete the Master of Divinity degree program, with the specific intention of seeking ordination. Their intent stems from a profound sense of God's call. Student spiritual formation, or the background and process out of which a student feels called to ministry, may take place from early childhood years to later years in life. However, over half the women entering New Brunswick Seminary first sensed a call to ministry between the ages of 31 and 50. Other Christian women had significant impact on their spiritual formation. The point at which these Christian women most influenced students occurred after the student was over thirty years of age.

Because of part-time enrollment, the length of time to complete the three year traditional Master of Divinity program is extended. Women attending part-time now normally take between 4 and 6 years to complete their Master of Divinity programs, although many women discover that the length of their seminary studies may extend beyond 6 years.[17]

For women studying at New Brunswick, employment outside the home is the rule rather than the exception. Three out of four women work at jobs outside the home, and over half of the women are engaged in full-time employment positions.[18]

The marital status of women seminarians today is varied. Although a clear majority are married and have been for some time, single, divorced,

16. The seminary's calendar currently follows a trimester format. A full course load would reflect between 9 and 12 credit hours. For spring, 1995, the number of credit hours covered a broad range extending from 3 to 17 credits. Eighteen of the women, or 43.7%, were taking between 6 and 9 credit hours. Twelve women were enrolled for more than 9 hours, and 11 women were enrolled for less than 6 hours.

17. When asked how many years they thought they would be taking classes at the time they first enrolled, about 3/4 of the women anticipated their studies would take between 4 and 6 years. The remaining 25% of the women were about equally divided between its taking the traditional 3 years and its taking between 7 and 9 years. When asked how long they now thought it would take them to complete the program, about half of the women found their studies will have taken between 5 and 6 1/2 years. From this we can say that, generally speaking, the women's study programs are taking one or two semesters longer than originally projected.

18. Just over 75% of the women worked outside the home, with 53% working in full time positions, and 23% working on a part time basis.

widowed, and partnered women are all present in New Brunswick's student body.[19] Among married students, almost 75% of the women decided to attend seminary after entering into the marriage relationship—not before.[20] Husbands/partners prove to be the greatest supporters of female seminarians, with children and parents supportive in decreasing degree.[21]

Among women seminarians today, most have children who live at home. The children range in age from two to nineteen.[22] The average child's age is 13. Because women are older when entering seminary, it can also be assumed that they with their partners increasingly contend with the health concerns of aging parents.

The degree of past and present involvement in their local churches by women seminarians cannot be overstated. With few exceptions, women bring to their seminary studies rich experience in the local church. This experience ranges from traditional women's roles to dynamic and creative church involvement with a growing involvement in prayer groups and "care" positions in congregations.[23]

Congregational and denominational support for women in the seminary varies within the broad number of church traditions represented in the student body. Almost all women feel encouraged by their local congregations.[24] Denominational encouragement is not as universally

19. Response to inquiry about marital status on the survey was optional, but all 49 women responded. Ten percent of the women have never married, 69% are married, 12% are divorced, 5% are widowed, and 5% are partnered. Of the 69% currently married, the marriage timespan runs from 1/2 year to 39 years, and the average marriage is 19 1/2 years in length.
20. In the survey 74% of the women indicated that they had not considered seminary before getting married.
21. With regard to ordination, 83% of the women felt they had the full support of their husbands or partners. Only one woman indicated no support from her spouse. Regarding parent support, 68% felt they had the full support of their parents. Two students felt no support from parents. Seventy-four percent indicated the full support of their children.
22. Although it would be helpful to learn the overall size of the womens' immediate families, a more relevant and useful survey question asked for the ages of children who presently live at home. Almost 82% of the women had children at home between 2 years and 19 years of age.
23. Among the RCA students, 45% had served on their consistories, and 27% do so presently.
24. In assessing support from their home congregations, 91% of the women felt they had congregational support.

received.[25] For RCA women, 86% feel the encouragement of the local church, and 75% perceive encouragement from the denomination.

When does the commitment of women to attend New Brunswick Seminary require personal sacrifice? The demands placed upon the typical woman seminarian are awesome. Were it not for her faith in Christ's leading, her understanding of the presence of the Holy Spirit in her life and her sense of call to preparation for greater Christian leadership, few if any women could withstand the stress and pressures of attending seminary today. Meeting essential needs and faithfully fulfilling commitments to spouses, to growing children, to aging parents, to employers, to neighbors and church friends, is daunting and stressful enough in any person's life. But added to these challenges emerge new demands on time, energy, and resources brought about by returning to the classroom and to the supervised ministry requirements of the M. Div. program. The sacrifices which each woman is compelled to make to complete the program involve not only her personal choices concerning time, energy and resources, but choices agreed to and supported by her spouse or partner, her children, and those others who also support her pursuit of ordination.

Because the typical female student coming to New Brunswick completed college almost twenty years earlier, returning to an academic environment is frightening. Coping with exams and writing academic papers with deadlines involves utilizing skills which she may or may not have used in years. She isn't always convinced she can meet the demands of the classroom.

This stress increases with worries about the demands of her job outside the home, which do not lessen in response to her commitment to attend classes at the seminary, and she worries about making ends meet.[26] If she

25. Perceived denominational support dropped to 70% among the total number surveyed. Two of the total number of women indicated no support at all from her denomination.
26. In attempting to identify the sources of their stress, the women were asked what kinds of stress limited their enjoyment of their seminary learning experience. The question was broken down into categories which included job demands, support from spouse, church and denomination, health — both their own and the health of another—child care, the demands of older children, household chores, concern for elderly parents, financial worries, anxiety over traveling to classes, and "other." In their responses, almost half the women indicated that the two greatest sources of stress are job-related stress and worry over money. About one quarter of the women identified child care, obtaining denominational support, and travel to and from classes as sources of anxiety and stress.

is an RCA student, the cost for nine credit hours (three coures) in 1998/99 is approximately $2,160, and for non-RCA students this cost approximates $2,250.

The working hours of her day and week need to be lengthened and carefully managed. Depending on her work schedule, she may take daytime classes. More likely, however, she takes all of her classes at night. This means driving in rush hour traffic to arrive in time for the first session of her class which begins at 6:20 p.m. She'll finish just before eight o'clock. The second session begins at eight thirty after chapel worship and a social break. She will get out of class at ten o'clock. Fortunately the average forty-minute drive home won't be made in rush hour traffic.

Since the typical student is most likely married and has been for some time, she feels the support and encouragement of her husband, but her seminary attendance has placed new demands on their marriage relationship. By the time she returns from her nighttime classes, she is fatigued, family needs demand attention, and there is little time to spend alone with her husband.

Because most women have children at home who may or may not be in school, arrangements must be made for their supper, their oversight, and of course, preparation for school the following day. She tries to keep the vows she made at the baptism of her children. She wants to be a good and loving parent — to meet the needs of her children in emotional and social as well as educational and physical ways.

In addition to the demands of work and family the typical woman seminarian is involved in her local church, where she may serve on the consistory or governing board. If not on consistory, she is involved in one or more forms of ministry or service within the congregation. She values the encouragement and support of her congregation, although her commitment to her church requires her time and energy.

Just as she is never sure how long it will take to drive to her 6:20 class in rush hour traffic, she is never sure how long it will take to do her assignments for classes — not to mention the thought of Greek and Hebrew language studies. The stress of not knowing is accompanied by her own need for a time of quiet reflection and prayer.

In what ways are these seminarians of today related to Rebecca Knox, Ann Hertzog, and Mary Board? What do they share in common?

I believe it fair to say that all are strong women who take their Christian faith seriously. They are visionaries who believe in the future and are willing to commit themselves to making the future better than the present. They have heard a word from the Lord and are willing to risk the comfort and security of the present for a more meaningful future. They believe in themselves and what it is they are doing. They are willing to risk personal failure by the choices they are making and to live with the anxiety and stress created by the choices they have made. They are concerned for the welfare of New Brunswick Theological Seminary and for what this institution can do to train learned and compassionate leaders for the future of Christ's Church.

For all Christians everywhere, faithfulness to the gospel carries a price, just as our Lord paid the price for our salvation. To give up something of and from ourselves on behalf of furthering the gospel message implies sacrificial giving. Rebecca Knox, Ann Hertzog, and Mary Board each made sacrifices in seeking to be faithful to the gospel message. So too do the women who attend New Brunswick Theological Seminary today, seeking to be faithful to their call to Christian leadership.

Contributors

John W. Beardslee III is Abraham Messler Quick Professor of Church History, emeritus, at New Brunswick Theological Seminary.

Elton J. Bruins is director of the A. C. Van Raalte Institute, and Evert J. and Hattie E. Blekkink Professor of Religion, emeritus, at Hope College in Holland, Michigan.

John W. Coakley is L. Russel Feakes Memorial Professor of Church History at New Brunswick Seminary.

Joyce Borgman de Velder is minister of the Old Saratoga Reformed Church in Schuylerville, New York.

Firth Haring Fabend, a historian, is a fellow of the Holland Society of New York.

Russell L. Gasero is archivist of the Reformed Church in America.

Joyce D. Goodfriend is professor of history at the University of Denver.

Carol W. Hageman, a life-long member of the Reformed Church in America, currently serves as an elder and as vice president of the consistory at the First Church in Albany, New York.

Renée S. House is academic dean and director of Gardner A. Sage Library at New Brunswick Theological Seminary.

Mary Kansfield is an independent scholar whose research and writing focus on the history of women in the United States.

Jennifer Mary Reece is a Ph.D. candidate in church history at Princeton Theological Seminary.

Karsten T. Rumohr-Voskuil is a student at Western Theological Seminary in Holland, Michigan.

Johan van de Bank is professor of Reformed church history, emeritus, at the University of Utrecht, the Netherlands.

Index

174